The Anti- Inflammatory Diet

Anti-Inflammatory Diet for Beginners, the Easy and Healthy Anti-Inflammatory Diet Recipes, Anti-Inflammatory Diet Plan, Cookbook Diet, Anti-Inflammatory Diet Weight Loss

By Marvin Hampton

derived from various sources. Please consult a licensed professional before attempting any techniques outlined in this book.

By reading this document, the reader agrees that under no circumstances is the author responsible for any losses, direct or indirect, that are incurred as a result of the use of the information contained within this document, including, but not limited to, errors, omissions, or inaccuracies.

Table of Contents

Part One: Treating Inflammatory Diseases Through An Anti-Inflammatory Diet 9

Chapter 1 – How to Prepare for a Lifestyle Change with an Anti-Inflammatory Diet 9

Chapter 2 – The Anti-Inflammatory Diet as a Medicine (The Science Behind the Anti-Inflammatory Diet) 12

What is Chronic Inflammation? 13

Causes and Symptoms 15

Symptoms of Chronic Inflammation 17

Is Chronic Inflammation Painful? 20

Chapter 3 – The Link Between Inflammatory Diseases and Diet 21

Foods to Eat..25

Dietary Approaches to Reduce Inflammation 28

The Role of Herbs..30

The Anti-Inflammatory Diet Pyramid 33

Chapter 4 – Start Living the Anti-Inflammatory Diet Lifestyle 36

Get Physical Exercise..36

Get Enough Sleep 37

Manage Stress 38

Manage Your Weight..39

Avoid Toxic Environments and Allergens 40

Benefits of Making Lifestyle Changes 41

Part Two: The Anti-Inflammatory Diet Recipes......42

Chapter 5 – Breakfast and Brunch 42

1. Quinoa and Black Beans 42

2. Lemon Avocado Toast 45

3. Protein Pancakes 47

4. Pumpkin Pancakes 49

5. Cinnamon Raisin Bread 51

6. Zucchini Noodle Breakfast Bowl 53

7. Baked Apples 56

8. Mashed Cauliflower...................................58

9. Broccoli-Turkey Brunch Casserole 60

10. Banana Bread...................................62

11. Pumpkin Protein Bowl 64

12. Baked French Toast Casserole...................................66

13. Whole Grain Blueberry Scones...................................69

Chapter 6 – Lunch...................................72

14. Grilled Avocado Sandwich 72

15. Cauliflower Steaks with Tamarind and Beans...................................74

16. Smoked Salmon Tartine...................................77

17. Healthy Chicken Marsala 80

18. Grilled Salmon Burgers 83

19. Tuna Steaks...................................85

20. Air Fryer Salmon 87

21. Rosemary Garlic Lamb Chops 89

22. Mushroom Farro Risotto 91

23. Instant Pot Black Beans 94

24. Popcorn Chicken 96

Chapter 7 – Snacks and Appetizers **99**

25. Spicy Tuna Rolls 99

26. Spicy Kale Chips 102

27. Cacao Coffee Protein Bars 104

28. Cauliflower Popcorn...106

29. Lemony Quinoa 108

30. White Beans with Pepper....................................110

31. Blueberry-Lemon Bread 112

Chapter 8 – Dinner 114

32. Shrimp and Vegetable Curry...............................114

33. Vegetable and Chicken Stir Fry............................116

34. Baked Tilapia with Rosemary and Pecan 118

35. Toasted Brown Rice with Thyme and Mushrooms....120

36. Italian Stuffed Peppers 123

37. Chicken with Herb Parmesan Spaghetti Squash........126

38. Chicken Curry with Tamarind & Pumpkins...............129

39. Zucchini and Lemon Herb Salmon 132

40. Parmesan and Lemon Fish 135

41. Chicken Lemon Piccata 137

42. Blackened Chicken Breast 140

43. Chicken Marrakesh..142

Chapter 9 – Salads and Soups...............................144

44. Hazelnut, Beetroot and Lentil 144

45. Chicken & Lentil Soup with Escarole, Parsnips 146

46. Lemon, Chicken & Kale Soup 148

47. Fennel Carrot Soup...151

48. Green Papaya Salad 154

49. Vegan Lentil Mushroom Salad 156

50. Mediterranean Spinach Tuna Salad 159

51. Chicken Tortilla Soup 161

52. Carrot Cucumber Salad 164

Chapter 10 – Desserts..................................**166**

53. Apple Cinnamon Chips 166

54. Lemon Vegan Cake 168

55. Dark Chocolate Granola Bars 171

56. Blueberry Crisp 173

57. Chocolate Chip Quinoa Granola Bars 175

58. Strawberry Granita 178

59. Apple Fritters...180

60. Roasted Bananas 182

Chapter 11 – Sides **184**

61. Parmesan Roasted Broccoli 184

62. Thyme with Honey-Roasted Carrots...................186

63. Roasted Parsnips 188

64. Green Beans...190

65. Roasted Carrots..192

Chapter 12 – Beverage and Broths.....................**194**

66. Turmeric and Apple Cider Vinegar Detox Tea.........194

67. Lemon Drop Mocktail....................................196

68. Celery Juice...198

69. Strawberry Green Tea 200

70. Raspberry Lemonade 202

Chapter 13 – Sauces and Dressing.....................**204**

71. Turmeric Tahini Dressing................................204

72. Anti-Inflammatory Salad Dressing......................206

73. Ginger & Turmeric Dressing 208

74. Strawberry Sauce 210

75. Coriander Chutney 212

Part Three: 2-Week Meal Plan **214**

Chapter 14 – Week 1 .... **215**

Chapter 15 – Week 2 .... **219**

Part Four: Tips for an Anti-Inflammatory Diet.....**223**

Chapter 16 – Top 15 Anti-Inflammatory Super
Foods **228**

Chapter 17 – Anti-Inflammatory Diet and
Intermittent Fasting. How to Combine the two.....**237**

What is Intermittent Fasting? 237

Does Intermittent Fasting Work................................239

What the Researchers Found...................................240

Benefits of Intermittent Fasting 240

Chapter 18 – Foods That Increase Inflammation **.242**

Does A Vegetarian Diet Reduce Inflammation? 245

BONUS: How to achieve Weight Loss with Anti-
Inflammatory Diet **247**

Weight Gain and Neurological Inflammation 249

APPENDIX A: **251**

Measurement Conversions **251**

Conclusion **252**

REFERENCES **253**

PART ONE: TREATING INFLAMMATORY DISEASES THROUGH AN ANTI-INFLAMMATORY DIET

CHAPTER 1 – HOW TO PREPARE FOR A LIFESTYLE CHANGE WITH AN ANTI-INFLAMMATORY DIET

Chronic inflammatory illnesses cause the most deaths around the world. The WHO(World Health Organization) has **reported** (1) that chronic diseases are the #1 threat to human health. Ironically, inflammation in the human body is actually good for us, as it protects and heals us. But the same process can cause problems when it spins out of control. The body ends up attacking itself, causing many health problems.

Chronic inflammation may cause diabetes, cardiovascular illnesses, arthritis, allergies, chronic obstructive pulmonary disease and many more.

Consider this...

The American Diabetes Association has reported 30.3 million or almost 10% of the population having diabetes, making it the 7th most common cause of death. The American Heart Association says there are 800,000 deaths every year in the country from cardiovascular diseases, which is 31% of all deaths. 60% of Americans are now suffering from at least one chronic condition. **Around the world, 66% of people die from a chronic inflammatory disease**.

So the chronic inflammatory condition cannot be ignored. Luckily, it can be cured, and the symptoms can also be reversed.

In this book, I will discuss the chronic inflammatory disease in detail, its causes, symptoms, and treatments. I will show how making simple food changes can help you prevent the disease and help you lead a healthier life. I will reveal the foods to eat and avoid. I will also discuss some lifestyle changes that can help you immensely.

Finally, I will provide **75 mouth-watering anti-inflammatory recipes**, all with a list of easily available ingredients, and a detailed step-by-step making process.

The anti-inflammatory diet you will find in this book will be a life-changer. You will eat better, stay healthy, live longer, and lead a more fulfilling, happier life.

Get ready for this positive change. I am sure this book is going to help you immensely.

Happy reading!

CHAPTER 2 – THE ANTI-INFLAMMATORY DIET AS A MEDICINE (THE SCIENCE BEHIND THE ANTI-INFLAMMATORY DIET)

Understanding Chronic Inflammation

Inflammation is a natural process within the human body. It is our defense mechanism to fight injuries, toxins, and infections. Imagine what would happen if we were left exposed to all the threats around us. So inflammation is good for us.

The body's immune system recognizes irritants, pathogens, and damaged cells, and releases chemicals to start the healing process. Proteins and antibodies are released. Blood flow also increases to the damaged parts of our bodies.

This is the body's natural biological response. The process can last from some hours to a few days, especially for acute inflammation. It can be uncomfortable sometimes, but it's a good thing because your body is trying to heal itself and protect you. Wounds, infections, and tissue damage cannot be healed without an inflammatory response.

Acute Inflammation

This is the body's first reaction, and it normally occurs within minutes. Acute inflammation is short-lived. Many mechanisms begin work to destroy the invaders and repair the damaged or dead cells. The affected area returns to balance and the inflammation will dissipate quickly in a few hours or days, depending on the nature of the attack or its intensity.

What is Chronic Inflammation?

Sometimes, however, this inflammation will persist for a long time, which will cause the body to remain in a constant state of alert. This condition can continue for months and even years, especially if the immune system is unable to remove the problem completely. **The condition when the inflammation continues even after it should end is called 'chronic inflammation'.**

Over time, chronic inflammation will do more harm than good. Chronic inflammation is known to be the **cause** (2) heart disease, rheumatoid arthritis, diabetes, asthma, Alzheimer's and even some types of **cancer** (3). For instance, those suffering from chronic inflammatory bowel diseases like Crohn's disease and ulcerative colitis have a higher risk of colon cancer.

According to the **findings** (4) of the National Cancer Institute, long-term chronic inflammation can even cause severe DNA damage.

There is bound to be a negative impact, if the human body is always on high alert. It will react to deal with it, even in instances where there is no real emergency.

For example, the presence of inflammatory cells in the blood vessels for long periods of time, will lead to the buildup of plaque. The arteries will thicken if the plaque keeps building up, which may cause a stroke or a heart attack.

Inflammation in the brain can also cause Alzheimer's disease. Scientific studies have revealed that the immune cells of our body can infiltrate our brains in times of distress.

Causes and Symptoms

Like we have discussed, chronic inflammation is triggered when the body perceives an internal threat, sometimes, even if there is no real disease or injury to fight. At other times, modern science is yet unsure as to why exactly the inflammation persists.

However, we do know that the condition can be caused by many factors, such as,

> ➢ An autoimmune disorder where the immune system attacks healthy tissues by mistake
> ➢ Long-term irritant exposure like polluted air or industrial chemicals
> ➢ Untreated acute inflammation causes, like an injury or infection

Factors like **obesity** (5), smoking, **chronic** stress (6), and alcohol abuse can also cause chronic inflammation according to some medical studies.

Eating packaged and processed foods that are loaded in trans fats may also promote inflammation and modify the endothelial cells lining the arteries. Vegetable oils used for making processed foods can also cause damage according to the **findings** (7) of this study. Many scientists believe that if you consume them regularly, then it can cause an imbalance in the level of omega-3 to omega-6 fatty acids in your body, which will promote inflammation.

Too much processed meat and excessive alcohol intake may also cause an inflammatory effect on the body.

There are non-dietary **causes** (8) too, such as leading an inactive or sedentary lifestyle. This can be one of the major causes according to some scientific reports.

What happens to the body when it is inflamed? There will be 3 main processes before and during the acute inflammation –

1. Branches of the arteries will get enlarged, thus allowing more blood flow to the damaged part.
2. Capillaries will make it easier for the proteins and fluids to infiltrate. So they will be able to move between the cells and blood easily.
3. The body will release neutrophils, a type of WBC or white blood cell that is full of small sacks containing digestive microorganisms and enzymes.

Symptoms of Chronic Inflammation

There are many symptoms of the condition. But they will always be different for each person, and the intensity will also vary. Here are some of the most common symptoms.

1. **Fatigue** – If you are always feeling tired, without any real reason, it could be because of chronic inflammation. This could be a sign that your body is battling out something. With inflammation, your body will ask for more **cellular energy** (9) so that the immune cells can be regenerated. This will further deplete the necessary fuel your body needs, thus making you feel even more tired.

   First, make sure that you are getting adequate sleep. You should be concerned if you are feeling tired even after this.

2. **Physical Pains** – Do you suffer from frequent pains and aches? Chronic pain can be a sign that you may have arthritis, which majorly contributes towards inflammation. Body pains like joint and muscle aches are often caused by systematic inflammation. High

levels of inflammatory cytokines in the body can attack joints and muscles, causing swelling, pain, and redness.

3. **Skin Rashes** – Rashes on the skin like psoriasis or **eczema** (10) are inflammatory skin issues that are characterized by rough, flaky, and red skin. Psoriasis and eczema have both been linked to a hypersensitive immune system. Those who suffer from these conditions have more inflammatory mast cells that can trigger skin rashes when activated.

   Even an acne breakout or a skin that is too dry could be a sign of chronic inflammation.

4. **Excess Mucus** – Feeling like blowing your nose or clearing your throat too often? It could be a sign that your body is inflamed. If the body feels it is inflamed, your mucous membranes will make thick phlegm to protect the epithelial cells, located in the lining of your respiratory system. This can cause a runny nose, sneezing, and constant coughing.

5. **Digestive Issues** – Constipation, abdominal pain, loose stool, and bloating are some common digestive problems for a lot of people. Chronic inflammation could be causing them. It can contribute to the leaking

gut **syndrome** (11), or permeability in the intestines that may cause toxins and bacteria to leak through the walls of your intestine to the rest of your body.

Be careful if you have a leaky gut because it can fuel systematic inflammation and cause digestive issues like irregular bowel movements and abdominal distention.

6. **Heartburn** – Be careful with heartburn as well. Clinical **studies** (12) carried out recently have revealed that GERD (Gastroesophageal Reflux Disease) is probably more from inflammation. Previously, it was believed that stomach acids traveling up from the esophagus was the cause of heartburn.

This study found that it was the human body's inflammatory response that was causing the pain and damage in the esophagus, eventually causing the heartburn. Further, treating the inflammation resulted in a reduction of the heartburn. The Journal of the American Medical Association published the findings of this study.

7. **Swollen Lymph Nodes** – The lymph nodes are mostly located in the neck region, close to the groin,

and below the armpits. They can swell up if there is a physical problem in the body. So it is essential to look out for them. They will swell if the body is raging a battle against infection, and will then return to normal once we are well again.

If these nodes are always inflamed, then it could be a sign of a constant struggle. It could be a symptom of an underlying issue or a chronic illness.

Is Chronic Inflammation Painful?

Chronic inflammatory symptoms are painful for many people. There can be stiffness, distress, discomfort, pain, and even agony. It all depends on how severe the symptoms are. The kind of pain can also vary. You may suffer from a steady and constant pain. It could be a pulsating and throbbing ache or a pain that seems to stab you.

There can be pain from inflammation mostly because of the swelling, which will push against your sensitive nerve endings. This will send the pain signals to your brain. There can be other biochemical processes as well. They will affect how the nerves in the body behave.

CHAPTER 3 – THE LINK BETWEEN INFLAMMATORY DISEASES AND DIET

Luckily, the right food choices you make can reduce the risk of chronic inflammation to a great extent. So a powerful way of combating inflammation does not come from the pharmacy but your grocery store. Several experimental studies have revealed that components of beverages and foods can have a very positive effect. In fact, food is probably one of the best ways of combating inflammation.

So how can we define an anti-inflammatory diet...

An anti-inflammatory diet is an eating plan that aims to reduce or prevent chronic inflammation in the human body, which can cause many severe medical conditions if left untreated.

The diet focuses on fresh vegetables and fruits. Many plant-based foods around us give us antioxidants. It also focuses on nuts, lean proteins, whole grains, healthy fats, spices, and seeds. The intake of alcohol, red meats, and processed foods is discouraged. So you have to avoid them or limit their intake as much as you can.

Remember the following –

> ➤ Vegetables and fruits have natural components known as phytonutrients, which can protect us against inflammation.
> ➤ Foods that have a lot of saturated fats can, on the other hand, increase inflammation. Also, foods containing trans fats and highly processed foods can also be inflammatory to your body.
> ➤ Healthy fats like omega-3 fatty acids and monounsaturated fats can help you stay away from chronic inflammation.

Also, make sure to achieve a good balance of carbs, protein, and fat in every meal you have. Your anti-inflammatory eating plan must also meet the requirements of your body by providing you with all the minerals, fiber, vitamins, and water you need.

Some foods can, however, trigger the creation of free radicals. For instance, foods like fries that are cooked by using the same heated oil again and again.

Dietary Antioxidants & Inflammation

They are molecules found in food that help you eradicate free radicals from your body. What are these free radicals? They are natural byproducts of bodily processes, which are produced by oxygen metabolism. External factors, like smoking and stress can also enhance the level of free radicals in your body.

These free radicals can cause cell damage, which boosts the risk of inflammation.

Your body makes some antioxidants that will help you get rid of these toxic substances. However, we still need dietary antioxidants. The right anti-inflammatory diet will increase the number of antioxidants in your body that will help you fight the free radicals.

Like, omega-3 fatty acids that you get from oily fish. Omega-3 can lower the inflammatory protein level in your body. The Arthritis Foundation has **found** (13) that fiber may also achieve the same effect.

So the right anti-inflammatory diet should contain nutrient-dense, whole foods with antioxidants. You should also avoid or limit processed foods.

The Mediterranean diet, where the focus is on healthy oils and plant-based foods, is considered to be anti-inflammatory. Several scientific studies have **revealed** (14) that the Mediterranean diet can lower the inflammatory markers like IL-6 and CRP.

A diet low in carbohydrates is also **effective** (15) in lowering inflammation, especially for people with metabolic syndrome or those who are overweight. Further, vegan and vegetarian diets have also been found to be very effective.

Anti-Inflammatory Diet Types

The Mediterranean diet is anti-inflammatory as discussed already. Moreover, one more diet that has proven effective is the DASH diet.

> ➤ Promoted by the National Heart, Lung, and Blood Institute of the United States, the DASH diet is rich in vegetables, fruits, low-fat dairy foods, and whole grains.

Its main purpose is to control and prevent hypertension and also to improve heart health. But this diet will also help you with inflammation, as it can cure many of these health conditions.

Foods to Eat

You should eat foods with a lot of antioxidants and avoid the ones that can cause inflammation. Many scientists and nutrition experts have suggested that our diet should consist of whole grains, fresh vegetables and fruits, fatty fish, plant-based proteins, spices, and herbs to prevent and control inflammation.

The foods you consume should have 3 things.

1. A lot of nutrients
2. Healthy fats
3. Many types of antioxidants provided good for the body

Here are the top foods to eat –

➢ **Veggies and fruits** – Eat different types of fruits and vegetables. Research has revealed that leafy greens, such as kale and spinach that are rich in vitamin K can curb inflammation. Cabbage and broccoli are also good. You can also have cauliflower and Brussels sprouts. The best fruits to have include different types of berries like raspberries, blueberries, and blackberries. The color in them is a kind of pigment, which will also help you. Cherries, apples, olives, avocados, and grapes are good for health too.

➢ **Whole grains** – Brown rice, whole-wheat bread, oatmeal, and other unrefined grains have a lot of fiber. They are all good for you.

➢ **Beans** – Beans will also give you plenty of fiber. Soybeans, lentils, pinto beans, split peas, and kidney beans all come loaded with healthy proteins. Chickpeas are also very good for health. Plus, they will provide you with a lot of anti-inflammatory substances and antioxidants.

➢ **Nuts** – Almonds, pistachios, cashews, walnuts, pecans, hazelnuts, and peanuts are all good for us. Nuts are a good source of vital nutrients, and can promote weight loss, lower the level of triglycerides and cholesterol, reduce the risk of type-2 diabetes, and even heart attack and stroke. They are loaded with healthy fats and are also known to **fight** (16) inflammation. But make sure to only have a handful daily, because too many can make the calories add up quickly.

- ➢ **Fish** – Consume fish at least two times a week. The best is oily fish like tuna, salmon, mackerel, herring, anchovies, and sardines that till give you a lot of omega-3 fatty acids.

- ➢ **Spices and herbs** – They will add flavor and antioxidants to your food. There is curcumin, a strong substance, which you will find in turmeric. Garlic is also good because it prevents the body from making things that increase inflammation. Ginger is also good for your health.

So, here are some foods you should have every week –

- ➢ Dark green vegetables
- ➢ Avocados
- ➢ Artichokes
- ➢ Apples
- ➢ Broccoli
- ➢ Sweet potatoes
- ➢ Beans like pinto, black beans, and red beans
- ➢ Nuts like almond, walnuts, hazelnuts, and pecans
- ➢ Dark chocolate with a minimum of 70% cocoa
- ➢ Whole grains like brown rice and oats
- ➢ Olive oil and olives

- ➢ Healthy fats from coconut oil
- ➢ Fatty fish like herring, sardines, salmon, anchovies, and mackerel
- ➢ Chili peppers and bell peppers
- ➢ Green tea
- ➢ Women can have up to 140 ml or 5 ounces of red wine a day. For men, this is 280 ml or 10 ounces

Dietary Approaches to Reduce Inflammation

Here are 5 approaches that can help you sort out this problem –

#1 – Half of your plate should be veggies and fruits

- ➢ Have fresh vegetables and fruits in every meal
- ➢ Make sure you have brightly colored fruits and veggies
  - • It is best to have fresh food, instead of frozen, canned, or dried. Only make sure that it has a low sodium content and there are no added sugars.

- Eat vegetables from all sub-groups. This includes orange, red, and dark green veggies, and also peas and beans.

#2 – Proteins

- ➢ Go easy on the proteins. Moderately active people should limit their protein intake to a maximum half lb. Get omega-3 from fatty fish twice a week. That will help.
- ➢ Have days when there should be no meat. Eat tempeh, tofu, and legumes like peas, lentils, and peas on your meatless days.
- ➢ Go for leaner proteins like skinless turkey or chicken, or lean cuts of pork and beef.
- ➢ Take fat-free or low-fat dairy products, such as yogurt and skim milk where the saturated fat content is lower.
- ➢ Lower the intake of processed foods like bacon, sausage, and deli meat.

#3 – Healthy Fats

- ➢ Eat monounsaturated fats that include olive, canola, and avocado oils.

- ➢ Consume foods with omega-3
  - Have a fatty fish like salmon 2-3 times in a week
  - For snacks, you can eat walnuts or similar nutty products
  - Toss hemp seeds, chia seeds and flaxseed into your salad.
- ➢ Lower the consumption of processed food containing high saturated fat and hydrogenated oils.

#4 – Whole Grains

- ➢ Opt for whole-grain cereals and flours often.
- ➢ Make sure that you have different types of whole grains like quinoa, brown rice, wheat berries and millet.

#5 – Fresh Spices and Herbs

- Make your dishes yummy by adding herbs.
- Experiment with different spices.

The Role of Herbs

Certain herbs can give you very good results.

30

Harpagophytum Procumbens

Known as the grapple plant, wood spider, or devil's claw, this is an herb from South Africa. It is close to the sesame plants. Many believe that this herb has anti-inflammatory properties.

Hyssop

It is mixed with some other herbs like licorice and used sometimes to treat lung conditions and inflammation. The hyssop herb is available as an essential oil.

But be careful, because it has caused convulsions in trials. There is no alternative to lifestyle modifications and the right food choices.

Ginger

This magical herb has more than a hundred years' history of treating people with constipation, dyspepsia, colic problems, rheumatoid arthritis, and those suffering from gastrointestinal issues.

Turmeric

Turmeric too has a long history of treating a variety of conditions like Alzheimer's disease, arthritis, and several inflammatory conditions. It is mostly because of the curcumin it contains. A lot of research is being carried out to know more about this. You can get turmeric naturally through food or take a curcumin supplement.

Cannabis

A cannabinoid is known as cannabichromene also has anti-inflammatory properties. But, you cannot take cannabis legally in many places.

The Anti-Inflammatory Diet Pyramid

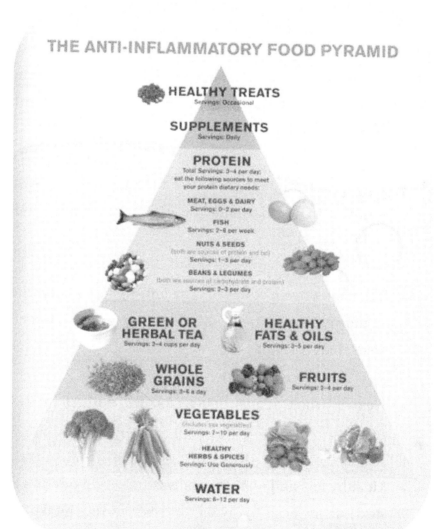

Developed by Dr. Andrew Weil, the famous integrative medicine expert from Harvard University, the anti-inflammatory food pyramid explains in detail which foods to eat and which to avoid. The pyramid makes it easier for us to understand the diet and follow it.

The pyramid is bottom-heavy, which means that the foods and beverages at the bottom are the most important. The importance reduces gradually as you climb the pyramid, with sweets or treats at the top.

> Water is at the bottom end of the pyramid. Dr. Weil stresses the importance of staying hydrated, and rightly so.

> Vegetables are just above. The anti-inflammatory diet is mostly plant-based. Eat plenty of fresh fruits and vegetables every day.

> Next is whole grains and fruits. Eat natural to stay healthy.

> Healthy fats and oils, especially extra-virgin olive oil is next. It is best to avoid or restrict the intake of vegetable oils.

➤ Dr. Weil has suggested that we eat 1 or 2 servings of protein daily. This mostly includes sea fish, which gives you healthy omega-3 fatty acids. You can also eat chicken as well as beans, legumes, nuts, and seeds which are all good for you. You can consume a variety of them with no problems at all. However, restrict the intake of eggs and milk products.

➤ The human body needs some supplements, but it is best to get the vital nutrients from natural sources as much as possible.

➤ Treats are at the topmost level of the pyramid, which means you should have them only occasionally. Dark chocolate with 70%+ cocoa content is good but avoid foods with artificial sweeteners.

CHAPTER 4 – START LIVING THE ANTI-INFLAMMATORY DIET LIFESTYLE

You must eat the right foods to beat chronic inflammation and avoid the diseases it causes. However, consuming only the the right food is never going to be enough. You may have to make some lifestyle modifications as well.

Here are some recommendations –

Get Physical Exercise

An active lifestyle is a healthy lifestyle. Studies have **shown** (17) that exercise can reduce inflammation. People who are into physical activities regularly show fewer inflammatory symptoms.

You should workout at least for half an hour a day, 5 days a week. That is a minimum. Better still if you do aerobic activities of moderate-intensity like playing tennis or brisk walking for an hour to 75 minutes or vigorous activities for 15 minutes in a day. Combine this with high-intensity muscle-strengthening activities like weight lifting a couple of days in a week.

Join a health club if you can. If you can't, then at least take up swimming classes or ride a bike to work. Don't use the escalator. Take the stairs instead. Every bit will help. Look for opportunities where you can sweat it out.

Get Enough Sleep

A lot happens when we sleep. The body repairs the organs, cells, tissues, and muscles. The chemicals that strengthen our immune systems circulate within the blood. Hormones are also made when we are asleep. Our bodies are fully repaired and recharged from sleep.

It is essential to get adequate sleep. It is very important to keep our minds and bodies healthy. According to The Center for Disease Control, 35% of all adults in the United States don't get the recommended 7 hours of **sleep** (18) every night, which can be dangerous. Poor quality sleep or not sleeping long enough can cause many health hazards, including type-2 diabetes, weight gain, and inflammation.

So make sure to sleep for at least 7 hours a night. Go to bed at 11 PM. Switch off all electronics and make the room dark. Also wear comfortable clothing, ensuring that nothing is bothering you as you are trying to doze off.

Manage Stress

There are different types of stress – physical (injuries), mental (financial), and emotional (relationship issues, sense of isolation, social rejection). We are all stressed to some extent. However, there is always a negative impact on the body if the stress becomes overwhelming.

The body will **lose** (19) its ability to respond if this stress is not relieved. You will begin to see the inflammatory symptoms and related diseases.

There are ways to manage stress efficiently like MBSR or Mindfulness-Based Stress Reduction, PMR or Progressive Muscle Relaxation techniques, and breathing exercises. You can also practice tai chi or yoga. Make it a habit of meditating for half an hour before going to bed. This will slow you down and help you relax. Take a break or go on a holiday if the stress seems too much.

Manage Your Weight

Obesity can be dangerous. It can cause diabetes, high blood pressure, osteoarthritis, breathing problems, gout, heart ailments, and even some types of cancer.

Research also suggests that obese people are more likely to have inflammation. Those who are overweight, especially in their abdominal area, are always at a higher risk. Adipocytes also known as the fat cells in the belly, produce and secrete compounds, which are known to cause inflammation.

Your immune system is under pressure if you have an excessive number of fat cells. It sees the fat cells as a 'foreign invader' and tries to fight them off, which turns on the inflammatory response. This becomes chronic over time.

Luckily, even a 10% **reduction** (20) in body weight will help you fight it off. An anti-inflammatory diet without sugar, little alcohol, and without red meat will help. Eating fewer calories and exercising will help you lose those extra pounds.

Avoid Toxic Environments and Allergens

To be honest, we cannot avoid toxins completely. But it will be very useful if you are aware of the environment you are in and avoid harmful materials as much as possible. This will help you reduce the inflammatory triggers.

Environmental toxins can cause cardiovascular diseases, diarrhea, chronic obstructive pulmonary disease, respiratory issues, and cancer, among others. Millions die around the world from toxins.

Food allergies can also be bad for health. Sadly, many people are not even aware of the different types of foods that can trigger allergies. So be careful. Try to identify the foods that are causing allergic reactions. Avoid them and you will see a difference. Similarly, try to avoid inhaling harmful toxins and chemicals.

Benefits of Making Lifestyle Changes

Few simple lifestyle changes can give you many benefits. Change to an anti-inflammatory diet, get enough sleep, reduce stress, and exercise. You will certainly see a marked improvement.

> You will see a reduced risk of diabetes, obesity, heart disease, cancer, and depression, among others.
> The symptoms of inflammatory bowel syndrome, arthritis, lupus, and several autoimmune diseases will improve.
> Inflammatory markers in the blood will go down.
> Markers for cholesterol, triglyceride, and blood sugar will improve.
> Your mood and energy levels will go up.

PART TWO: THE ANTI-INFLAMMATORY DIET RECIPES

CHAPTER 5 – BREAKFAST AND BRUNCH

1. Quinoa and Black Beans

Prep Time: *15 minutes/***Cook Time**: *35 minutes/*
Serves: *10*

Ingredients:

- ➤ 1 teaspoon of olive oil
- ➤ 3 garlic cloves, chopped
- ➤ 1 chopped onion
- ➤ 1-1/2 cups of vegetable broth
- ➤ ¾ cup quinoa
- ➤ ¼ teaspoon of cayenne pepper
- ➤ 1 teaspoon cumin, ground
- ➤ 1 cup corn kernels
- ➤ ½ cup cilantro, chopped
- ➤ 2 black beans, rinsed & drained
- ➤ Black pepper and salt to taste

Instructions:

1. Heat oil in your saucepan over medium temperature.
2. Stir cook the garlic and onion for 10 minutes.
3. Now mix your quinoa into the onion mix.
4. Cover with the vegetable broth.
5. Season with cayenne pepper, cumin, pepper, and salt.
6. Boil the mixture. Bring down the heat and keep it covered.
7. Let it simmer for 20 minutes.
8. Stir in the corn into your saucepan. 5 minutes.
9. Mix in the cilantro and black beans.

Nutrition Facts Per Serving

- ➢ Calories 162
- ➢ Carbohydrates 28g
- ➢ Cholesterol 0mg
- ➢ Total Fat 2g
- ➢ Protein 8g
- ➢ Sugar 2g

2. Lemon Avocado Toast

Prep Time: *10 minutes/****Cook Time:*** *3 minutes/****Serves:*** *2*

Ingredients:

- ½ avocado
- 2 slices of whole-grain bread
- ¼ teaspoon lemon zest
- 1 teaspoon lemon juice
- 2 tablespoons of cilantro, chopped
- 1 pinch of cayenne pepper
- ¼ teaspoon chia seeds
- 1 pinch of sea salt

Instructions:

1. Toast the slices of bread to your desired crispiness.

2. Mash the avocado in a mid-sized bowl.

3. Stir in the cilantro, lemon zest, lemon juice, cayenne pepper, and the sea salt.

4. Now spread the avocado mix on the toast.

5. Add the chia seeds on top.

Nutrition Facts Per Serving

➢ *Calories 69*

➢ *Carbohydrates 12g*

➢ *Cholesterol 0mg*

➢ *Total Fat 1g*

➢ *Protein 3g*

➢ *Sugar 2g*

3. Protein Pancakes

Prep Time: *5 minutes/****Cook Time:*** *5 minutes/****Serves:*** *2*

Ingredients:

- ½ lb. blueberries
- 1 scoop of vanilla protein powder
- 1 tablespoon of stevia
- ½ teaspoon of baking powder
- ¼ cup of water
- Sugar-free syrup

Instructions:

1. Blend all your ingredients together.

47

2. Place a pan on your stove. Apply some cooking spray.

3. Pour the pancake batter once your pan is hot. The layer should be thin.

4. Spread evenly.

5. Cook both sides for a minute.

6. Drizzle some sugar-free syrup

7. Serve with the berries.

Nutrition Facts Per Serving

- *Calories 106*
- *Cholesterol 5mg*
- *Total Fat 2g*
- *Fiber 2g*
- *Protein 22g*
- *Sugar 2g*

4. Pumpkin Pancakes

Prep Time: *5 minutes/**Cook Time:** 5 minutes/**Serves:** 1*

Ingredients:

> - 1/5 lb. egg whites
> - 1-1/2 tablespoon whole wheat flour
> - 1 oz. pumpkin puree
> - ½ teaspoon cinnamon
> - 1 scoop of protein collagen peptides
> - 2 teaspoons of stevia

Instructions:

1. Mix everything in a blender. Make it smooth.
2. Apply cooking spray on your pan. Heat over medium temperature.
3. Pour 1/3rd of the batter into your pan. Spread evenly.
4. Cook for 2 minutes. The edges should be light brown.
5. Flip over and cook for another 2 minutes.
6. Sprinkle stevia on top before serving.

Nutrition Facts Per Serving

➢ *Calories 165*
➢ *Cholesterol 0mg*
➢ *Carbohydrates 16g*
➢ *Total Fat 1g*
➢ *Fiber 3g*
➢ *Protein 23g*
➢ *Sugar 2g*

5. Cinnamon Raisin Bread

Prep Time: *20 minutes/****Cook Time:*** *30 minutes/*
Serves: *16*

Ingredients:

- ➢ 2 teaspoon cinnamon, ground
- ➢ 5 cups of whole wheat flour
- ➢ 1 package nutritional yeast
- ➢ 1-1/2 teaspoon salt
- ➢ 3 tablespoons of melted coconut oil
- ➢ 2 tablespoons of agave nectar
- ➢ 1 egg, beaten lightly

- ➢ 1 cup of skim milk
- ➢ 2/3 cup raisins

Instructions:

1. Apply cooking spray on a loaf pan.
2. Sift the flour, cinnamon, and salt in a mixing bowl.
3. Stir the raisins, agave, and yeast in. Create a well at the center.
4. Heat the skim milk and coconut oil in your saucepan and pour them into this well.
5. Add your beaten egg. Prepare a soft dough by mixing together.
6. Shape dough into a loaf. Keep in the pan. Cover with plastic wrap or towel.
7. Let it rise. In the meantime, preheat your oven to 425 degrees F.
8. Uncover your loaf. Brush milk on top.
9. Bake for 30 minutes. Let it cool before serving.

Nutrition Facts Per Serving

- ➢ *Calories 207*
- ➢ *Cholesterol 19mg*
- ➢ *Carbohydrates 38g*
- ➢ *Total Fat 3g*
- ➢ *Fiber 6g*
- ➢ *Protein 7g*
- ➢ *Sugar 8g*

6. Zucchini Noodle Breakfast Bowl

Prep Time: 15 minutes/**Cook Time:** 35 minutes/**Serves:** 2

Ingredients:

- ➢ 4 teaspoon of olive oil
- ➢ 2 parsnips, chopped
- ➢ 2 garlic cloves, chopped
- ➢ ½ avocado, chunked
- ➢ 1 teaspoon lemon juice
- ➢ 3 zucchinis
- ➢ 1 pinch black pepper and sea salt
- ➢ 2 eggs

➤ 2 green onions, chopped

Instructions:

1. Preheat your oven to 375 degrees F.
2. Keep the parsnips on your baking sheet. Drizzle half a teaspoon of oil.
3. Bake for 25 minutes. Set aside.
4. Keep the garlic, avocado, water, and the remaining oil in your blender.
5. Blend well and keep aside.
6. Now cut the zucchini into strips lengthwise.
7. Turn each strip slightly. Discard the cores. Set aside.
8. Pour water into your saucepan. Boil over medium heat.
9. Add the lemon juice. Bring down the heat to a slow boil.
10. Now break the eggs in a small bowl.
11. Cook for 5 minutes until the whites set completely. The yolks should start to thicken.
12. Lift eggs gently from the water. Keep them warm.
13. Boil water over high temperature. Bring down the heat to medium.
14. Cook the zucchini for 3 minutes. Take out from the heat.

15. Transfer to a serving bowl. Season with pepper and salt.

16. Now add the avocado mix. Blend well by tossing gently.

17. Divide your zucchini into two bowls.

18. Top with green onions, an egg, and parsnips.

Nutrition Facts Per Serving

- ➤ *Calories 362*
- ➤ *Cholesterol 183mg*
- ➤ *Carbohydrates 37g*
- ➤ *Total Fat 18g*
- ➤ *Fiber 10g*
- ➤ *Protein 13g*
- ➤ *Sugar 13g*

7. Baked Apples

*Prep Time: 5 minutes/**Cook Time:** 60 minutes/**Serves:** 6*

Ingredients:

- ➢ 6 apples, cored & halved
- ➢ 2 cups of sugar-free orange carbonated beverage

Instructions:

1. Preheat your oven to 350 degrees F.
2. Place apples on a baking dish.
3. Cut the sides that face down.
4. Now pour your orange beverage over the apples.

5. Bake for an hour. The apples should become tender.

Nutrition Facts Per Serving

> ➢ *Calories 64*
> ➢ *Cholesterol 0mg*
> ➢ *Carbohydrates 15g*
> ➢ *Total Fat 0g*
> ➢ *Fiber 2g*
> ➢ *Protein 1g*
> ➢ *Sugar 11g*

8. Mashed Cauliflower

Prep Time: *5 minutes/**Cook Time:*** *10 minutes/**Serves:*** *6*

Ingredients:

- ➢ 1 cauliflower head
- ➢ 1/8 cup melted coconut oil
- ➢ 1 red chili, diced
- ➢ 1 mango, sliced
- ➢ ½ chopped onion
- ➢ 1 garlic clove, optional

> Salt and pepper
> Paprika to taste

Instructions:

1. Steam the cauliflower till it becomes tender.
2. You can steam with a garlic clove as well.
3. Now cut your cauliflower into small pieces.
4. Keep the coconut oil in your blender.
5. Season with pepper and salt. Whip until it gets smooth.
6. Pour the cauliflower into a small baking dish. Sprinkle the paprika.
7. Bake in the oven till it becomes bubbly.

Nutrition Facts Per Serving

> Calories 64
> Carbohydrates 12g
> Total Fat 0g
> Protein 4g
> Fiber 5g
> Sodium 91mg
> Sugars 5g

9. Broccoli-Turkey Brunch Casserole

Prep Time: *10 minutes/**Cook Time:** 15 minutes/**Serves:** 6*

Ingredients:

- ➢ 2-1/2 cups turkey breast, cubed and cooked
- ➢ 1 lb. broccoli, chopped and drained
- ➢ 1-1/2 cups of coconut milk
- ➢ 1 cup almond paste
- ➢ 10 oz. cream of chicken soup. low sodium and low fat
- ➢ ½ lb. egg substitute
- ➢ ¼ teaspoon of poultry seasoning
- ➢ ¼ cup of sour cream, low fat
- ➢ ½ teaspoon pepper

- ➢ 1/8 teaspoon salt
- ➢ 2 cups of seasoned stuffing cubes

Instructions:

1. Bring together the egg substitute, soup, coconut milk, pepper, sour cream, salt, and poultry seasoning in a big bowl.
2. Now stir in the broccoli, turkey, ¾ cup of the paste and stuffing cubes.
3. Transfer to a baking dish. Apply cooking spray.
4. Bake for 10 minutes. Sprinkle the remaining almond paste.
5. Bake for another 5 minutes.
6. Keep it aside for 5 minutes. Serve.

Nutrition Facts Per Serving

- ➢ *Calories 299*
- ➢ *Carbohydrates 26g*
- ➢ *Fiber 3g*
- ➢ *Sugar 8g*
- ➢ *Cholesterol 72mg*
- ➢ *Total Fat 7g*
- ➢ *Protein 33g*

10. Banana Bread

Prep Time: *15 minutes/****Cook Time:*** *45 minutes/****Serves:*** *8*

Ingredients:

- ➤ ¾ cup whole wheat flour
- ➤ 2 medium ripe mashed bananas
- ➤ 2 large eggs
- ➤ 1 teaspoon of Vanilla extract
- ➤ ¼ teaspoon baking soda
- ➤ ½ cup stevia

Instructions:

1. Keep parchment paper at the bottom of your pan. Apply some cooking spray.

2. Whisk together the baking soda, salt, flour, and cinnamon (optional) in a bowl.

3. Keep it aside.

4. Take another bowl and bring together the eggs, bananas, and vanilla in it.

5. Stir the wet ingredients gently into your flour mix. Combine well.

6. Now pour your batter into the pan. You can also sprinkle some walnuts.

7. Heat your air fryer to 310°F. Cook till it turns brown.

8. Keep the bread on your wire rack so that it cools in the pan. Slice.

Nutrition Facts Per Serving

> *Calories 240*
> *Carbohydrates 29g*
> *Total Fat 12g*
> *Protein 4g*
> *Fiber 2g*
> *Sodium 184mg*
> *Sugar 17g*

11. Pumpkin Protein Bowl

Ingredients:

- ➢ ½ lb. pumpkin, already baked
- ➢ 1 banana, sliced
- ➢ 1/10 lb. protein powder scoop
- ➢ ¼ cup blueberries
- ➢ ¼ cup raspberries

Instructions:

1. Grate the pumpkin.

2. Stir in the protein powder. Combine well.

3. Now layer the banana slices, blueberries, and raspberries.

4. You can add toppings like nuts, hemp hearts, and chia seeds.

Nutrition Facts Per Serving

- ➤ *Calories 348*
- ➤ *Carbohydrates 67g*
- ➤ *Cholesterol 0mg*
- ➤ *Total Fat 2g*
- ➤ *Protein 28g*
- ➤ *Fiber 19g*
- ➤ *Sodium 8mg*
- ➤ *Sugar 24g*

12. Baked French Toast Casserole

Prep Time: *20 minutes/****Cook Time:*** *45 minutes/****Serves:*** *12*

Ingredients:

- ➢ 1 lb. French bread
- ➢ 1 cup of egg white liquid
- ➢ 6 eggs
- ➢ 1/3 cup maple syrup
- ➢ 1-1/2 cups of rice milk,
- ➢ ½ lb. raspberries

- ½ lb. blueberries
- 1 teaspoon of vanilla extract
- ¾ cup strawberries

Instructions:

1. Slice the bread into small cubes. Keep them in a greased casserole dish.
2. Add all the berries. Only leave a few for the topping.
3. Whisk together the egg whites, eggs, rice milk, and maple syrup in a bowl.
4. Combine well.
5. Pour the egg mix over the top of the bread. Press the bread down. All pieces should be soaked well.
6. Add berries on the top. Fill up the holes, if any.
7. Refrigerate covered for a couple of hours at least.
8. Take out the casserole half an hour before baking.
9. Set your oven to 350 degrees F.
10. Now, bake your casserole uncovered for 30 minutes.
11. Bake for another 15 minutes covered with a foil.
12. Let it rest for 15 minutes.
13. Serve it warm with maple syrup.

Nutrition Facts Per Serving

- ➢ Calories 200
- ➢ Carbohydrates 31g
- ➢ Cholesterol 93mg
- ➢ Total Fat 4g
- ➢ Protein 10g
- ➢ Fiber 2g
- ➢ Sodium 288mg
- ➢ Sugar 10g

13. Whole Grain Blueberry Scones

Prep Time: *10 minutes/****Cook Time:*** *25 minutes/****Serves:*** *8*

Ingredients:

- ➢ 2 cups of whole-wheat flour
- ➢ ¼ cup maple syrup
- ➢ 6 tablespoons of olive oil
- ➢ 2-1/2 teaspoons baking powder
- ➢ ½ teaspoon see salt
- ➢ 2 tablespoons of coconut milk

- ➤ 1 teaspoon vanilla extract
- ➤ 1 cup blueberries

Instructions:

1. Preheat your oven to 400 degrees F. Keep parchment paper on your baking sheet.
2. Add the syrup, flour, salt, and baking powder in a bowl. Combine well by whisking together.
3. Pour the olive oil into a bowl with the dry ingredients.
4. Work the oil into your flour mix.
5. Stir the vanilla extract and coconut milk into the dry ingredients bowl.
6. Fold in the blueberries gently. Your dough should be sticky and thick.
7. Apply some flour to your hands and shape the dough into a circle.
8. Take a knife and create triangle slices.
9. Keep them on the baking sheet. Maintain an 8-inch gap.
10. Bake for 25 minutes. Set aside on the baking sheet for cooling once done.

Nutrition Facts Per Serving

- ➤ Calories 331
- ➤ Carbohydrates 27g
- ➤ Cholesterol 0mg
- ➤ Total Fat 23g
- ➤ Protein 4g
- ➤ Fiber 4g
- ➤ Sugar 8g

CHAPTER 6 – LUNCH

14. Grilled Avocado Sandwich

Prep Time: *10 minutes/***Cook Time***: 15 minutes/***Serves:** *4*

Ingredients:

- ➢ 8 slices of pumpernickel bread
- ➢ 1 cup sauerkraut, drained & rinsed
- ➢ 1 cup hummus
- ➢ 1 teaspoon dairy-free margarine

- ➤ 1 avocado, peeled & sliced into 16 pieces

Instructions:

1. Preheat your oven to 450 degrees F.

2. Apply margarine on one side of your bread slices.

3. Keep 4 slices on your baking sheet. The margarine side should be down.

4. Distribute half of the hummus over the bread slices.

5. Place sauerkraut on the hummus.

6. Keep avocado slices over your sauerkraut.

7. Spread hummus on the remaining slices.

8. Keep the hummus side down on your slices of avocado.

9. Bake for 7 minutes.

10. Flip over and bake for another 6 minutes.

Nutrition Facts Per Serving

- ➤ *Calories 340*
- ➤ *Carbohydrates 39g*
- ➤ *Total Fat 16g*
- ➤ *Protein 10g*
- ➤ *Fiber 11g*
- ➤ *Sugar 1g*
- ➤ *Sodium 781mg*
- ➤ *Potassium 552mg*

15. Cauliflower Steaks with Tamarind and Beans

Prep Time: 20 minutes/**Cook Time:** 50 minutes/**Serves:** 2

Ingredients:

- ½ cup of olive oil
- 1/5 lb. cauliflower head
- 1 teaspoon black pepper, ground
- 2 teaspoons of kosher salt
- 3 cloves of garlic, chopped
- ½ lb. green beans, trimmed
- 1/3 cup parsley, chopped
- ¾ teaspoon lemon zest, grated

- ➢ 1/5 lb. parmesan, grated
- ➢ ¼ lb. panko breadcrumbs
- ➢ 1/3 cup tamarind
- ➢ 1 lb. white beans, rinsed & drained
- ➢ 1 teaspoon of Dijon mustard
- ➢ 2 tablespoons of margarine

Instructions:

1. Preheat your oven to 425 degrees F.
2. Take out the leaves and trim the stem ends of your cauliflower.
3. Keep the core side down on your working surface.
4. Slice from the center top to down with a knife.
5. Keep it on a baking sheet.
6. Apply 1 tablespoon oil on both sides. Season with pepper and salt.
7. Roast for 30 minutes. Turn halfway through.
8. Toss the green beans in the meantime with 1 tablespoon of oil and pepper.
9. Keep on your baking sheet in a single layer.
10. Roast for 15 minutes.
11. Whisk the lemon zest, garlic, parsley, salt, pepper, and oil together in a bowl.
12. Keep half of this mix in another bowl.

13. Add Parmesan and panko to the first bowl. Use your hands to mix.

14. Add tamarind and white beans to the second bowl. Coat well by tossing.

15. Now whisk together the mustard and margarine.

16. Spread your margarine mix over the cauliflower.

17. Sprinkle the panko mix over the cauliflower.

18. Add the white bean mix to the sheet with beans. Combine.

19. Keep sheet in the oven and roast for 5 minutes.

20. Divide the beans, cauliflower, and tamarind among plates.

Nutrition Facts Per Serving

- Calories 1366
- Carbohydrates 166g
- Cholesterol 6mg
- Total Fat 67g
- Protein 59g
- Fiber 41g
- Sugar 20g
- Sodium 2561mg

16. Smoked Salmon Tartine

*Prep Time: 20 minutes/**Cook Time:** 20 minutes/**Serves:** 2*

Ingredients:

- ➤ 1/3 pumpkin
- ➤ 2 tablespoons of dairy-free margarine
- ➤ 1-1/2 tablespoons chives, minced
- ➤ ¼ lb. cashew paste
- ➤ Thinly sliced smoked salmon
- ➤ ½ clove of garlic, minced
- ➤ ½ lemon zest
- ➤ 2 tablespoons red onion, chopped
- ➤ 2 tablespoons capers, drained

- ➤ ½ boiled egg, chopped
- ➤ Black pepper and kosher salt

Instructions:

1. Bring together the lemon zest, garlic and cashew paste in a bowl.
2. Season with pepper and salt. Stir in the chives gently and set aside.
3. Now season the boiled egg and red onion with salt.
4. Grate your pumpkin.
5. Squeeze the pumpkin and remove any excess liquid. Season with pepper and salt.
6. Heat the margarine over medium temperature.
7. Add the pumpkin. Use a spatula to shape roughly into a circle.
8. Use the backside of a spoon to press on your mixture.
9. Cook covered for 10 minutes.
10. Flip and cook for another 8 minutes. It should be crispy and golden brown.
11. Take out and let it cool.
12. Spread the paste mix on top.
13. Layer your smoked salmon over this.
14. Sprinkle with capers, the boiled egg, and red onion.

15. Garnish with chives.

16. Cut into small wedges before serving.

Nutrition Facts Per Serving

- ➢ *Calories 734*
- ➢ *Carbohydrates 37g*
- ➢ *Cholesterol 115mg*
- ➢ *Total Fat 54g*
- ➢ *Protein 25g*
- ➢ *Sugar 3g*
- ➢ *Fiber 5g*
- ➢ *Sodium 1641mg*

17. Healthy Chicken Marsala

Prep Time: 15 minutes/Cook Time: 30 minutes/Serves: 4

Ingredients:

- ➤ 1-1/2 chicken breasts, boneless & skinless
- ➤ 2 tablespoons of dairy-free margarine
- ➤ ½ lb. shiitake mushrooms, sliced & stemmed
- ➤ 1 lb. baby Bella mushrooms, sliced & stemmed
- ➤ 2 tablespoons of extra virgin olive oil
- ➤ 3 cloves of garlic, chopped

80

- ➢ 1 cup shallot, chopped
- ➢ 2 cups of chicken broth, low-sodium
- ➢ ¾ cup dry marsala wine
- ➢ Black pepper, kosher salt, chopped parsley leaves

Instructions:

1. Dry your chicken breasts using a paper towel.
2. Slice them horizontally into half.
3. Keep each piece between parchment paper. Use your meat mallet to pound until you have ¼ inch thickness.
4. Season all sides with black pepper and kosher salt.
5. Dredge in some whole wheat flour. Keep aside.
6. Heat your skillet over medium temperature.
7. Pour olive oil and margarine in your pan.
8. Sauté the chicken for 5 minutes. Work in batches, not overcrowding your pan.
9. Transfer to a baking sheet. Set aside.
10. Wipe off excess cooking fat from your pan. Bring back to heat.
11. Add the remaining margarine and the mushrooms.
12. Sauté over high temperature. Season with black pepper and salt.
13. Add the garlic and chopped shallot to your pan.

14. Sauté 3 minutes. Include the marsala wine. Bring down the heat for a minute.

15. Include the chicken broth and cook for 5 minutes.

16. Transfer chicken cutlets to the pan. Spoon over the sauce.

17. Garnish with parsley.

Nutrition Facts Per Serving

- ➢ Calories 546
- ➢ Carbohydrates 41g
- ➢ Cholesterol 31mg
- ➢ Total Fat 38g
- ➢ Protein 10g
- ➢ Sugar 6g
- ➢ Fiber 5g
- ➢ Sodium 535mg

18. Grilled Salmon Burgers

Prep Time: 10 minutes/**Cook Time:** 10 minutes/**Serves:** 4

Ingredients:

- ➤ 1 lb. salmon fillet, skinless and cubed
- ➤ 1 tablespoon Dijon mustard
- ➤ 1 tablespoon lime peel, grated
- ➤ 1 tablespoon ginger, peeled & minced
- ➤ 1 tablespoon cilantro, chopped
- ➤ 1 teaspoon soy sauce, low-sodium
- ➤ ½ teaspoon coriander, ground

- ➤ Cilantro leaves and lime wedges
- ➤ Pepper and salt to taste

Instructions:

1. Preheat your barbecue grill on medium heat.
2. Apply cooking spray on the grill's rack lightly.
3. Pulse the salmon in your food processor. It should grind coarsely.
4. Take out the salmon and keep in a bowl.
5. Mix in the lime peel, mustard, cilantro, ginger, coriander, and soy sauce.
6. Create 4 patties.
7. Season with pepper and salt.
8. Grill your burgers, turning once on medium heat. 4 minutes for each side.
9. Garnish with cilantro leaves and lime wedges.

Nutrition Facts Per Serving

- ➤ *Calories: 395*
- ➤ *Cholesterol: 60 mg*
- ➤ *Carbohydrates: 1 g*
- ➤ *Fat: 7 g*
- ➤ *Sugar: 0 g*
- ➤ *Fiber: 0 g*
- ➤ *Protein: 23 g*

19. Tuna Steaks

Prep Time: *15 minutes/****Cook Time:*** *15 minutes/****Serves:*** *2*

Ingredients:

- ➤ 1-1/2 cups water
- ➤ 1 tablespoon lemon juice
- ➤ Pepper and salt to taste
- ➤ 1 teaspoon cayenne pepper
- ➤ 2 tuna steaks
- ➤ 3 kumquats, seeded, sliced, rinsed
- ➤ 1/3 cup cilantro, chopped

Instructions:

1. Mix lemon juice, cayenne pepper and water over medium heat in a saucepan.

2. Season with pepper and salt. Boil.

3. Now include the tuna steaks into this mix.

4. Sprinkle cilantro and kumquats.

5. Cook for 15 minutes. The fish should flake easily with your fork.

Nutrition Facts Per Serving

➢ *Calories: 141*

➢ *Cholesterol: 50 mg*

➢ *Carbohydrates: 6 g*

➢ *Fat: 1 g*

➢ *Sugar: 3 g*

➢ *Fiber: 2 g*

➢ *Protein: 27 g*

20. Air Fryer Salmon

Prep Time: *6 minutes/****Cook Time:*** *5 minutes/****Serves:*** *2*

Ingredients:

- ➢ 1/3 lb. filets of salmon
- ➢ ¼ cup of margarine
- ➢ ¼ cup of pistachios, chopped finely
- ➢ 1-1/2 tablespoons of minced dill
- ➢ 2 tablespoons of lemon juice

Instructions:

1. Preheat your air fryer to 400 degrees F.
2. Spray olive oil on the basket.

3. Season your salmon with pepper to taste. You can also apply the all-purpose seasoning.

4. Combine the margarine, lemon juice, and dill in a bowl.

5. Pour a spoonful on the fillets.

6. Top the fillets with chopped pistachios. Be generous.

7. Spray olive oil on the salmon lightly.

8. Air fry your fillets now for 5 minutes.

9. Take out the salmon carefully with a spatula from your air fryer.

10. Keep on a plate. Garnish with dill.

Nutrition Facts Per Serving

- *Calories 305*
- *Carbohydrates 1g*
- *Cholesterol 43mg*
- *Total Fat 21g*
- *Protein 28g*
- *Fiber 2g*
- *Sugar 3g*
- *Sodium 92mg*

21. Rosemary Garlic Lamb Chops

Prep Time: *3 minutes*/**Cook Time:** *10 minutes*/**Serves:** *2*

Ingredients:

- ➢ 4 chops of lamb
- ➢ 1 teaspoon olive oil
- ➢ 2 teaspoon garlic puree
- ➢ Fresh garlic
- ➢ Fresh rosemary

Instructions:

1. Keep your lamb chops in the fryer grill pan.

2. Season the chops with pepper and salt. Brush some olive oil.

3. Add some garlic puree on each chop.

4. Cover the grill pan gaps with garlic cloves and rosemary sprigs.

5. Refrigerate to marinate.

6. Take out after 1 hour. Keep in the fryer and cook for 5 minutes.

7. Use your spatula to turn the chops over.

8. Add some olive oil and cook for another 5 minutes.

9. Set aside for a minute.

10. Take out the rosemary and garlic before serving.

Nutrition Facts Per Serving

- *Calories 678*
- *Carbohydrates 1g*
- *Cholesterol 257mg*
- *Total Fat 38g*
- *Protein 83g*
- *Sugar 0g*
- *Sodium 200mg*

22. Mushroom Farro Risotto

*Prep Time: 15 minutes/**Cook Time:** 60 minutes/**Serves:** 5*

Ingredients:

- ➢ 3 tablespoons of melted coconut oil
- ➢ 4 cups chicken broth, low sodium
- ➢ ¾ lb. baby Bella mushrooms, trimmed & sliced
- ➢ ½ yellow onion, chopped
- ➢ 3 cloves of garlic, chopped
- ➢ 1 tablespoon thyme, chopped
- ➢ ¾ cup of dry white wine
- ➢ 1-1/2 cups organic farro

- ➢ 1 teaspoon lemon juice
- ➢ ¾ cup vegan parmesan
- ➢ ¾ cup peas
- ➢ Ground black pepper, kosher salt, chopped parsley

Instructions:

1. Keep your chicken broth in a saucepan. Simmer over low heat.
2. Heat the coconut oil over medium temperature in a pot.
3. Add kosher salt and onion. Sauté for 6 minutes. Stir often.
4. Bring up the heat to high. Now add the mushrooms. Combine by stirring.
5. Cook for another 2 minutes. The mushrooms should become soft.
6. Add the thyme and garlic. Sauté for a minute, stirring occasionally.
7. Include the toast and farro and cook for 1 more minute. Keep stirring.
8. Pour in the white wine. Cook for 3 minutes. Stir often. The wine needs to be absorbed completely.
9. Add the hot broth to your pot. Combine well.

10. Bring down the heat and cook for 45 minutes. Stir every 15 minutes.

11. Add the lemon juice and grated parmesan. Stir to combine.

12. Fold in the peas. Season with pepper and salt.

13. Take out the pot from heat. Let it sit covered for 5 minutes.

14. Garnish with thyme leaves and parsley.

Nutrition Facts Per Serving

➢ *Calories 397*

➢ *Carbohydrates 29g*

➢ *Cholesterol 32mg*

➢ *Total Fat 25g*

➢ *Protein 14g*

➢ *Sugar 5g*

➢ *Fiber 5g*

➢ *Sodium 429mg*

23. Instant Pot Black Beans

Prep Time: *15 minutes/***Cook Time:** *15 minutes/***Serves:** *8*

Ingredients:
- ➤ 2 cups of black beans, rinsed & dried
- ➤ 1 yellow onion, chopped
- ➤ 2 tablespoons of extra virgin olive oil
- ➤ 2 garlic cloves, smashed
- ➤ 1 jalapeno pepper, sliced
- ➤ 1 yellow or red bell pepper, stemmed & seeded
- ➤ 1 handful of cilantro

- ½ teaspoon of red pepper flakes
- 2 teaspoons cumin, ground
- 2 teaspoons kosher salt

Instructions:

1. Keep the black beans in your saucepan. Cover with cold water for 6 hours.
2. Drain and rinse.
3. Heat oil and add the garlic, onions, and salt. Sauté for 5 minutes.
4. Add the jalapeno, bell pepper, red pepper flakes, black pepper, and cumin.
5. Sauté for another 3 minutes. Stir frequently.
6. Now include the cilantro stems, beans, water, and some more salt. Combine well by stirring. Cook for 7 minutes. Release naturally.

Nutrition Facts Per Serving

- *Calories 144*
- *Carbohydrates 14g*
- *Cholesterol 0mg*
- *Total Fat 8g*
- *Protein 4g*
- *Sugar 1g*
- *Fiber 4g*
- *Sodium 606mg*

24. Popcorn Chicken

Prep Time: 15 minutes/Cook Time: 10 minutes/Serves: 4

Ingredients:

> 1/5 lb. chicken breast halves, boneless and skinless

> ½ teaspoon paprika

> ¼ teaspoon mustard, ground

> ¼ teaspoon of garlic powder

> 3 tablespoons of arrowroot

Instructions:

1. Cut the chicken into small pieces and keep in a bowl.

2. Combine the paprika, garlic powder, mustard, salt, and pepper in another bowl.

96

3. Reserve a teaspoon of your seasoning mixture. Sprinkle the other portion on the chicken. Coat evenly by tossing.

4. Combine the reserved seasoning and arrowroot in a plastic bag.

5. Combine well by shaking.

6. Keep your chicken pieces in the bag. Seal it and shake for coating evenly.

7. Now transfer the chicken to a mesh strainer. Shake the excess arrowroot.

8. Keep aside for 5-10 minutes. The arrowroot should start to get absorbed into your chicken.

9. Preheat your air fryer to 390 degrees F.

10. Apply some oil on the air fryer basket.

11. Keep the chicken pieces inside. They should not overlap.

12. Apply cooking spray.

13. Cook until the chicken isn't pink anymore.

Nutrition Facts Per Serving

- ➤ Calories 156
- ➤ Carbohydrates 6g
- ➤ Cholesterol 65mg
- ➤ Total Fat 4g
- ➤ Protein 24g
- ➤ Sugar 0g
- ➤ Fiber 1g
- ➤ Sodium 493mg

CHAPTER 7 – SNACKS AND APPETIZERS

25. Spicy Tuna Rolls

Prep Time: *10 minutes/****Cook Time:*** *10 minutes/****Serves:*** *6*

Ingredients:

- ➢ 6-1/2 tablespoons of wild-caught tuna
- ➢ 1 cucumber
- ➢ 1/16 teaspoon cayenne, ground
- ➢ 2 slices of diced avocado

- ➢ 1/8 teaspoon pepper
- ➢ 1/8 teaspoon salt
- ➢ 1 teaspoon hot sauce
- ➢ 12 toothpicks

Instructions:

1. Slice the cucumber lengthwise. Make thin cuts.
2. Flip the cucumber and slice the opposite side.
3. Discard the outermost slices. There should be no seeds.
4. Take a paper towel and pat dry. Set aside.
5. Keep the tuna, cayenne, hot sauce, pepper, and salt in a mixing bowl.
6. Combine well. Everything should mix well.
7. Spoon out the tuna mix across the cucumber slices. Leave an inch on each side.
8. Keep an avocado on top of your tuna.
9. Roll up the cucumber. Use toothpicks to secure the ends.

Nutrition Facts Per Serving

- ➢ *Calories 129*
- ➢ *Carbohydrates 2g*
- ➢ *Total Fat 9g*
- ➢ *Protein 10g*
- ➢ *Fiber 1g*

26. Spicy Kale Chips

Prep Time: *5 minutes/**Cook Time:*** *20 minutes/**Serves:*** *4*

Ingredients:

- ➢ 1 bunch kale
- ➢ ¼ teaspoon cayenne pepper, ground
- ➢ 1/8 teaspoon black pepper
- ➢ ¼ teaspoon of sea salt
- ➢ 1/8 teaspoon garlic powder

Instructions:

1. Preheat your oven to 300 degrees F.
2. Tear the kale leaves from their stems or ribs. The sizes should be of potato chips.
3. Keep them on a wire baking rack on a cookie sheet, lined with foil.
4. Apply cooking spray lightly. Some on your hands.
5. Massage the kale leaves lightly.
6. Sprinkle cayenne pepper, garlic powder, and salt.
7. Bake for 20 minutes. The edges should be crispy.

Nutrition Facts Per Serving

- ➤ *Calories 34*
- ➤ *Carbohydrates 3g*
- ➤ *Total Fat 2g*
- ➤ *Protein 1g*
- ➤ *Sugar 1g*
- ➤ *Sodium 156mg*
- ➤ *Potassium 139mg*

27. Cacao Coffee Protein Bars

Prep Time: *10 minutes/****Cook Time:*** *10 minutes/****Serves:*** *12*

Ingredients:

- ➤ 1 cup of egg white protein powder
- ➤ 2 cups of nuts (walnuts, cashews, pecans, or almonds)
- ➤ 3 tablespoons instant coffee
- ➤ ¼ cup of cocoa powder
- ➤ 18 dated, pitted
- ➤ 4 tablespoons of water

Instructions:

1. Use parchment paper to line your pan. Set aside.

2. Process the egg white protein, nuts, coffee powder, and cocoa powder in a bowl. The nuts should break down into small pieces.

3. Add the pitted dates. Process to combine well.

4. Process until you see the mixture becoming sticky.

5. Stir the cocoa nibs in.

6. Transfer the mixture to your pan. Press into the pan evenly with your hands.

7. Refrigerate for an hour. Cut into squares with a knife.

Nutrition Facts Per Serving

- ➤ *Calories 280*
- ➤ *Carbohydrates 23g*
- ➤ *Cholesterol 0mg*
- ➤ *Total Fat 16g*
- ➤ *Protein 11g*
- ➤ *Sugar 16g*
- ➤ *Fiber 4g*
- ➤ *Sodium 104mg*

28. Cauliflower Popcorn

Prep Time: *5 minutes/***Cook Time**: *30 minutes/***Serves:** *1*

Ingredients:

- ➢ 4 cups of cauliflower, cut into florets
- ➢ 1 teaspoon of olive oil
- ➢ Salt to taste

Instructions:

1. Core and cut your cauliflower florets.

2. Toss with the oil. Coat well.

3. Sprinkle with salt.

4. Roast at 450 degrees F for 30 minutes. They should become brown and tender.

5. Drizzle extra-virgin olive oil and serve.

6. You can also add dressing on top.

Nutrition Facts Per Serving

➤ *Calories 121*

➤ *Carbohydrates 10g*

➤ *Total Fat 5g*

➤ *Protein 4g*

➤ *Fiber 4g*

29. Lemony Quinoa

***Prep Time:** 15 minutes/**Cook Time:** 10 minutes/**Serves:** 6*

Ingredients:

- ➤ ¼ cups pine nuts
- ➤ 1 cup quinoa
- ➤ ¼ cup lemon juice
- ➤ Sea salt to taste
- ➤ 2 chopped celery stalks
- ➤ ¼ chopped red onion
- ➤ ¼ teaspoon cayenne pepper
- ➤ ½ teaspoon cumin, ground
- ➤ 1 parsley bunch, chopped

Instructions:

1. Keep pine nuts in a skillet and toast over medium temperature.
2. Stir. Keep aside for cooling.
3. Combine water, salt and the quinoa in your saucepan.
4. Boil. Bring down the heat.
5. Cook till the quinoa has become tender. Water must be absorbed.
6. Let it cool. Use a fork to fluff.
7. Transfer to your serving bowl.
8. Stir the lemon juice, pine nuts, onion, celery, parsley, cumin, and cayenne pepper in.
9. Add some pepper and salt if required before serving.

Nutrition Facts Per Serving

- ➤ *Calories 117*
- ➤ *Cholesterol 0mg*
- ➤ *Carbohydrates 21g*
- ➤ *Fat 1g*
- ➤ *Sugar 1g*
- ➤ *Fiber 3g*
- ➤ *Protein 6g*

30. White Beans with Pepper

Prep Time: 10 minutes/*Cook Time:* 15 minutes/**Serves:** 4

Ingredients:

- ➢ 1 teaspoon extra-virgin olive oil
- ➢ ¼ chopped onion
- ➢ 1 chopped bull horn (yellow gypsy) sweet pepper
- ➢ 1 lb. beans, drained
- ➢ 1 pinch oregano, dried
- ➢ Salt to taste
- ➢ Ground cayenne pepper and black pepper to taste

Instructions:

1. Heat oil over medium temperature in your skillet.

2. Stir in the sweet pepper and onion.

3. Cook till it becomes tender.

4. Include the beans.

5. Now season with cayenne pepper, oregano, black pepper, and salt.

6. Keep cooking while stirring sometimes till the beans are adequately heated.

Nutrition Facts Per Serving

➤ *Calories 154*

➤ *Cholesterol 0mg*

➤ *Carbohydrates 26g*

➤ *Fat 2g, Sugar 2g*

➤ *Fiber 6g*

➤ *Protein 8g*

31. Blueberry-Lemon Bread

Prep Time: *10 minutes/****Cook Time:*** *1 hour/****Serves:*** *16*

Ingredients:

- ➢ 2 teaspoons of baking powder
- ➢ 1-1/2 cups of whole-wheat flour
- ➢ 2 teaspoons of arrowroot powder
- ➢ ½ teaspoon salt
- ➢ ½ cup olive oil
- ➢ 1 cup organic stevia
- ➢ ½ teaspoon vanilla

- ➢ 1 teaspoon of lemon zest
- ➢ 1 cup of blueberries

Instructions:

1. Preheat your oven to 350 degrees F.
2. Bring together 1 cup of flour, salt, and baking powder in a bowl.
3. Whisk together the stevia, arrowroot, lemon zest, vanilla, and oil. Blend well.
4. Now add to your flour mixture. Blend well by stirring.
5. Toss the blueberries with the remaining flour. Stir into the batter gently.
6. Pour this into your floured and greased loaf pan.
7. Bake for an hour.
8. Set aside for 10 minutes to cool.

Nutrition Facts Per Serving

- ➢ *Calories 200*
- ➢ *Carbohydrates 24g*
- ➢ *Cholesterol 45mg*
- ➢ *Total Fat 14g*
- ➢ *Protein 3g*
- ➢ *Sugar 14g*
- ➢ *Fiber 1g*
- ➢ *Sodium 150mg*

CHAPTER 8 – DINNER

32. Shrimp and Vegetable Curry

Prep Time: *5 minutes/***Cook Time:** *10 minutes/***Serves:** *4*

Ingredients:

- ➤ 1 sliced onion
- ➤ 3 tablespoons of olive oil
- ➤ 2 teaspoons of curry powder
- ➤ 1 cup of coconut milk
- ➤ 1 cauliflower
- ➤ 1 lb. shrimp tails

Instructions:

1. Add the onion to your oil.

2. Sauté to make it a bit soft.

3. Steam your vegetables in the meantime.

4. Add the curry seasoning, coconut milk, and spices if you want once the onion has become soft.

5. Cook for 2 minutes.

6. Include the shrimp. Cook for 5 minutes.

7. Serve with the steamed vegetables.

Nutrition Facts Per Serving

- *Calories 491*
- *Carbohydrates 11g*
- *Cholesterol 208mg*
- *Total Fat 39g*
- *Protein 24g*
- *Sugar 3g*
- *Fiber 5g*
- *Sodium 309mg*

33. Vegetable and Chicken Stir Fry

Prep Time: *5 minutes/***Cook Time***: 15 minutes/***Serves:** *6*

Ingredients:

> 3 tablespoons of olive oil

> 3 chicken breasts

> 3 medium zucchini or yellow squash

> 2 onions

> 1 teaspoon of garlic powder

> 1 broccoli

> 1 teaspoon basil

> 1 teaspoon of pepper and salt

Instructions:

1. Chop the vegetables and chicken.

2. Heat your skillet over medium temperature.

3. Pour olive oil and add the chicken. Cook while stirring.

4. Include the seasonings if you want.

5. Add the vegetables. Keep cooking until it gets slightly soft. Add the onions first and broccoli last.

Nutrition Facts Per Serving

- ➢ *Calories 183*
- ➢ *Carbohydrates 9g*
- ➢ *Cholesterol 41mg*
- ➢ *Total Fat 11g*
- ➢ *Protein 12g*
- ➢ *Sugar 4g*
- ➢ *Fiber 3g*
- ➢ *Sodium 468mg*

34. Baked Tilapia with Rosemary and Pecan

Prep Time: *10 minutes/***Cook Time:** *17 minutes/***Serves:** *4*

Ingredients:

- 1/3 cup of whole-wheat panko breadcrumbs
- 1/3 cup raw pecans, chopped
- ½ teaspoon of agave nectar
- 2 teaspoons of rosemary, chopped
- 1 pinch of cayenne pepper
- 1-1/2 teaspoon of olive oil
- ¼ lb. tilapia fillets, 4 pieces

- ➢ 1 egg white
- ➢ 1/8 teaspoon of salt

Instructions:

1. Preheat your oven to 350 degrees F.
2. Stir together the breadcrumbs, pecans, agave, rosemary, cayenne pepper, and salt in a baking dish.
3. Pour the olive oil. Toss and coat the mixture. Bake for 7 minutes.
4. Now increase the temperature to 400 degrees F.
5. Apply cooking spray on a glass baking dish. Whisk your egg white in a dish.
6. Dip the fish in the egg, and then into your pecan mix. One fish fillet at a time. Coat each side lightly.
7. Keep the fish fillets in your baking dish.
8. Keep the remaining pecan mix on the fillets. Bake for 10 minutes.

Nutrition Facts Per Serving

- ➢ *Calories 244*
- ➢ *Carbohydrates 7g*
- ➢ *Cholesterol 55mg*
- ➢ *Total Fat 12g*
- ➢ *Protein 27g*
- ➢ *Sugar 1g*
- ➢ *Fiber 2g*
- ➢ *Sodium 153mg*

35. Toasted Brown Rice with Thyme and Mushrooms

Prep Time: *10 minutes/****Cook Time:*** *50 minutes/****Serves:*** *3*

Ingredients:

- ½ chopped yellow onion
- 1-1/2 teaspoons of olive oil
- 1 cup of brown rice
- 2 cloves of garlic, minced
- ½ lb. crimini mushrooms, sliced
- 1 cup of vegetable broth

120

- ➢ 3 tablespoons parsley, minced
- ➢ 1 tablespoon thyme, minced
- ➢ 1 cup of water
- ➢ ¼ teaspoon ground pepper and salt

Instructions:

1. Heat half teaspoon of olive oil in your saucepan on medium heat.
2. Add the onion. Cook for 5 minutes. Add garlic. Cook for 1 more minute.
3. Now include the rice. Cook for a minute while stirring.
4. Stir the vegetable broth in along with the water. Boil and then reduce the heat.
5. Cook for 35 minutes. The liquid should be absorbed.
6. Heat a teaspoon of oil in a nonstick skillet on medium temperature.
7. Include the mushrooms. Cook for 4 minutes.
8. Stir the thyme in. Cook for a minute.
9. Add the parsley, mushrooms, pepper, and salt to your rice. Combine well.

Nutrition Facts Per Serving

- ➤ *Calories 62*
- ➤ *Carbohydrates 9g*
- ➤ *Total Fat 2g*
- ➤ *Protein 2g*
- ➤ *Sugar 1g*
- ➤ *Fiber 1g*
- ➤ *Sodium 202mg*

36. Italian Stuffed Peppers

Prep Time: *10 minutes/**Cook Time:** 50 minutes/**Serves:** 6*

Ingredients:

- ➤ ½ onion, chopped
- ➤ 1 tablespoon of olive oil
- ➤ ½ teaspoon of kosher salt
- ➤ 1 carrot, diced into ¼ inch thickness
- ➤ 1 teaspoon of Italian seasoning
- ➤ 3 garlic cloves, minced
- ➤ 3 cups of pumpkin, grated
- ➤ ½ teaspoon of red pepper flakes

- 1-1/4 cups of cooked quinoa
- 1 lb. chickpeas, drained and rinsed
- 3 red bell pepper, cut, remove the seeds and membrane
- ¼ cup parsley, minced
- ¼ cup of vegan Parmesan, grated

Instructions:

1. Preheat your oven to 350 degrees F.
2. Heat olive oil in your nonstick skillet over medium temperature.
3. Now add the carrots and onions.
4. Season with a little bit of salt. Cook for 5 minutes, stirring occasionally.
5. Stir the Italian seasoning, red pepper flakes, and garlic in. Cook for another minute.
6. Add the chickpeas, pumpkin, and the remaining salt. Boil and simmer for 8 minutes.
7. Remove from heat. Stir 3 tablespoons of parsley and the cooked quinoa in.
8. Keep the pepper in your baking dish. The cut side should be up.
9. Now divide your chickpea mix between the peppers evenly.

10. Pour half of the water to your baking dish.

11. Use a foil to cover tightly for 30 minutes. The peppers should be tender.

12. Sprinkle the parmesan over each pepper.

13. Bake uncovered for 5 minutes.

14. Garnish with the remaining parsley.

Nutrition Facts Per Serving

➢ Calories 276
➢ Carbohydrates 40g
➢ Cholesterol 6mg
➢ Total Fat 8g
➢ Protein 11g
➢ Sugar 6g
➢ Fiber 8g
➢ Sodium 612mg

37. Chicken with Herb Parmesan Spaghetti Squash

Prep Time: *15 minutes*/**Cook Time:** *20 minutes*/**Serves:** *4*

Ingredients:

- ➢ 1 lb. chicken breast, skinless & boneless, cut into small pieces
- ➢ 3 lb. spaghetti squash
- ➢ 2 teaspoons of olive oil
- ➢ 3 tablespoons shallots, minced
- ➢ 1 tablespoon of melted coconut oil

- ½ teaspoon rosemary, dried
- ½ teaspoon oregano, dried
- ½ teaspoon thyme, dried
- 3 cloves of garlic, minced
- ¼ teaspoon of ground pepper
- ¼ teaspoon of kosher salt
- 2 tablespoons parsley, minced
- 1/3 cup vegan Parmesan, grated
- ½ cup of chicken broth
- Pepper and salt to taste

Instructions:

1. Pierce your spaghetti squash with a knife in many places.
2. Keep it in a baking dish. Cook in your microwave for 12 minutes on high heat. Turn the spaghetti halfway through. Set aside.
3. Cut it in half along the length. Remove the fibers and seeds.
4. Twist the strands out with a fork. Keep in a bowl.
5. Heat your nonstick skillet over medium temperature.
6. Apply cooking spray lightly. Add the chicken.
7. Cook while stirring occasionally.
8. Transfer chicken to a bowl once done. Keep it aside.

9. Now bring down the heat to medium. Add the coconut oil and olive oil.

10. Include the shallots. Cook for 3 minutes.

11. Stir the rosemary, garlic, oregano, and thyme in.

12. Cook for another minute, while stirring.

13. Now stir the chicken broth in.

14. Let your mixture simmer for a couple of minutes.

15. Include your cooked chicken and spaghetti squash to the skillet.

16. Toss with your sauce.

17. Add the parsley and Parmesan. Toss once more.

Nutrition Facts Per Serving

- *Calories 295*
- *Carbohydrates 12g*
- *Cholesterol 80mg*
- *Total Fat 15g*
- *Protein 28g*
- *Sugar 5g*
- *Fiber 3g*
- *Sodium 557mg*

38. Chicken Curry with Tamarind & Pumpkins

Prep Time: *10 minutes/**Cook Time:** 35 minutes/**Serves:** 4*

Ingredients:

- ➤ 1 teaspoon of olive oil
- ➤ 8 chicken thighs, boneless & skinless, trimmed
- ➤ 1 onion, chopped
- ➤ ¾ teaspoon pepper, ground
- ➤ ½ teaspoon of salt
- ➤ 2 cups pumpkins, diced

- ➢ 3 garlic cloves, minced
- ➢ ¼ lb. tamarind, pulped
- ➢ 1-1/2 teaspoons coriander, ground
- ➢ 1-1/2 teaspoons of curry powder
- ➢ 1-1/2 teaspoons cumin, ground
- ➢ ¼ cup parsley, minced
- ➢ 1-1/4 cup chicken broth, fat-free
- ➢ Pepper and salt to taste

Instructions:

1. Season your chicken thighs (both sides) with half of the pepper and salt.
2. Heat your nonstick skillet over medium temperature.
3. Apply cooking spray lightly.
4. Add the chicken. Cook each side for 2 minutes. Transfer to a plate.
5. Heat olive oil in a skillet. Add the garlic and onions. Cook for 3 minutes.
6. Stir together the curry powder, pumpkin, tamarind, cumin, coriander, chicken broth, ¼ teaspoon pepper, and ¼ teaspoon salt in your skillet.
7. Boil the mixture and reduce heat to medium.
8. Let it simmer for 12 minutes. Stir occasionally.
9. Include the chicken. Cook covered for 15 minutes.

10. Cook uncovered for 10 minutes.

11. Stir the parsley in.

Nutrition Facts Per Serving

- ➤ *Calories 757*
- ➤ *Carbohydrates 52g*
- ➤ *Cholesterol 249mg*
- ➤ *Total Fat 29g*
- ➤ *Protein 86g*
- ➤ *Sugar 40g*
- ➤ *Fiber 8g*
- ➤ *Sodium 750mg*

39. Zucchini and Lemon Herb Salmon

Prep Time: *15 minutes/****Cook Time:*** *20 minutes, **Serves:** 4*

Ingredients:

- ➢ 2 tablespoons of olive oil
- ➢ 4 chopped zucchinis
- ➢ 2 tablespoons of lemon juice
- ➢ 2 tablespoons of agave nectar
- ➢ 2 garlic cloves, minced

- ➢ 1 tablespoon of Dijon mustard
- ➢ ½ teaspoon oregano, dried
- ➢ ½ teaspoon dill, dried
- ➢ ¼ teaspoon rosemary, dried
- ➢ ¼ teaspoon thyme, dried
- ➢ 4 salmon fillets
- ➢ 2 tablespoons parsley leaves, chopped
- ➢ Ground black pepper and kosher salt to taste

Instructions:

1. Preheat your oven to 400 degrees F.
2. Apply cooking spray on your baking sheet lightly.
3. Whisk together the lemon juice, brown sugar, dill, garlic, Dijon, rosemary, thyme, and oregano in a bowl.
4. Season with pepper and salt to taste. Set aside.
5. Keep the zucchini on your baking sheet in one single layer.
6. Drizzle some olive oil. Season with pepper and salt.
7. Add the fish in one layer. Brush each fillet with your herb mix.
8. Keep in the oven. Cook for 17 minutes.
9. Garnish with parsley and serve.

Nutrition Facts Per Serving

- ➤ *Calories 355*
- ➤ *Carbohydrates 15g*
- ➤ *Cholesterol 78mg*
- ➤ *Total Fat 19g*
- ➤ *Protein 31g*
- ➤ *Sugar 12g*
- ➤ *Fiber 2g*
- ➤ *Sodium 132mg*

40. Parmesan and Lemon Fish

Prep Time: 15 minutes/***Cook Time:*** 10 minutes/***Serves:*** 2

Ingredients:

- ➢ 4 tilapia fillets
- ➢ ¼ cup cornflakes, crushed
- ➢ 2 tablespoons of vegan Parmesan, grated
- ➢ 2 teaspoons vegan dairy-free butter, melted
- ➢ 1/8 teaspoon black pepper, ground
- ➢ ½ teaspoon lemon peel, shredded
- ➢ Lemon wedges

Instructions:

1. Heat your oven to 450 °F.

2. Rinse and then dry the fish using paper towels.

3. Apply cooking spray on your baking pan.

4. Now roll up your fish fillets. Start from their short ends.

5. Keep in the baking pan.

6. Bring together the vegan butter, Parmesan, corn flakes, pepper and lemon peel in a bowl.

7. Sprinkle the crumb mix on your fish roll-ups.

8. Press the crumbs lightly into the fish.

9. Bake for 6-8 minutes. The fish should flake easily with your fork.

10. Serve with lemon wedges.

Nutrition Facts Per Serving

➢ *Calories 191*

➢ *Cholesterol 71mg*

➢ *Carbohydrates 7g*

➢ *Fat 7g*

➢ *Sugar 1g*

➢ *Fiber 0g*

➢ *Protein 25g*

41. Chicken Lemon Piccata

Prep Time: *10 minutes/****Cook Time:*** *20 minutes/****Serves:*** *4*

Ingredients:

- ➢ 2 chicken breasts, skinless & boneless
- ➢ 2 tablespoons dairy-free margarine
- ➢ 1-1/2 tablespoons whole wheat flour
- ➢ ¼ teaspoon salt
- ➢ ¼ teaspoon white pepper
- ➢ 1/3 cup white wine, dry
- ➢ 2 tablespoons olive oil
- ➢ ¼ cup lemon juice
- ➢ 1/3 cup chicken stock, low-sodium

- ➤ ¼ cup minced Italian parsley
- ➤ ¼ cup capers, drained
- ➤ Pepper and salt to taste

Instructions:

1. Cut in half each chicken breast.

2. Spread your flour on a plate thinly. Season with pepper and salt.

3. Dredge the breast slices lightly in your seasoned flour. Set aside.

4. Heat your sauté pan over medium temperature.

5. Add the breast slices to your pan when you see the oil simmering.

6. Cook for 3 to 4 minutes.

7. Turn over the chicken slices.

8. Take out the slices. Set aside.

9. Add wine to the pan. Stir. Scrape up those browned bits from the bottom.

10. Now add the chicken stock and lemon juice.

11. Go to high heat. Boil till you have a thick sauce.

12. Bring down the heat. Stir the parsley and capers in.

13. Add back the breast slices to your pan. Rewarm.

Nutrition Facts Per Serving

- ➢ *Calories 227*
- ➢ *Cholesterol 72mg*
- ➢ *Carbohydrates 3g*
- ➢ *Fat 15g*
- ➢ *Fiber 1g*
- ➢ *Sugar 0g*
- ➢ *Protein 20g*

42. Blackened Chicken Breast

Prep Time: *10 minutes/****Cook Time:*** *15 minutes/****Serves:*** *2*

Ingredients:

- ➢ 2 chicken breast halves, skinless and boneless
- ➢ 1 teaspoon thyme, ground
- ➢ 2 teaspoons of paprika
- ➢ 2 teaspoons olive oil
- ➢ ½ teaspoon onion powder

Instructions:

1. Combine the thyme, paprika, onion powder, and salt together in your bowl.

2. Transfer the spice mix to a flat plate.

3. Rub olive oil on the chicken breast. Coat fully.

4. Roll the chicken pieces in the spice mixture. Press down, ensuring that all sides have the spice mix.

5. Keep aside for 5 minutes.

6. In the meantime, preheat your air fryer to 360 degrees F.

7. Keep the chicken in the air fryer basket. Cook for 8 minutes.

8. Flip once and cook for another 7 minutes.

9. Transfer the breasts to a serving plate. Serve after 5 minutes.

Nutrition Facts Per Serving

➤ *Calories 424*

➤ *Carbohydrates 3g*

➤ *Cholesterol 198mg*

➤ *Total Fat 11g*

➤ *Protein 79g*

➤ *Sugar 1g*

➤ *Fiber 2g*

➤ *Sodium 516mg*

43. Chicken Marrakesh

Prep Time: *25 minutes*/**Cook Time:** *4 hours*/**Serves:** *8*

Ingredients:

- ➢ 1 slice onion
- ➢ 2 garlic cloves, minced
- ➢ ½ lb. pumpkins
- ➢ 2 carrots, diced & peeled
- ➢ 1 lb. garbanzo beans, drained & rinsed
- ➢ ½ teaspoon cumin, ground
- ➢ 2 lbs. chicken breasts, skinless, halved, cut into small pieces

- ➤ ¼ teaspoon cinnamon, ground
- ➤ ½ teaspoon turmeric, ground
- ➤ ½ teaspoon black pepper, ground
- ➤ 1 teaspoon salt
- ➤ 1 teaspoon parsley, dried
- ➤ ½ lb. tamarind, pulped

Instructions:

1. Keep the garlic, onion, pumpkin, carrots, chicken breast and garbanzo beans in your slow cooker.
2. Mix turmeric, cumin, black pepper, cinnamon, salt and parsley in your bowl.
3. Sprinkle over the vegetables and chicken.
4. Add the tamarind. Combine well by stirring.
5. Keep your cooker covered. Set the heat to high.
6. Cook for 4 hours. The sauce should be thick.

Nutrition Facts Per Serving

- ➤ *Calories 520*
- ➤ *Carbohydrates 59g*
- ➤ *Cholesterol 101mg*
- ➤ *Fat 15g*
- ➤ *Fiber 13g*
- ➤ *Sugar 25g*
- ➤ *Protein 45g*
- ➤ *Sodium 424mg*

CHAPTER 9 – SALADS AND SOUPS

44. Hazelnut, Beetroot and Lentil

Prep Time: 10 minutes/**Cook Time:** 5 minutes/**Serves:** 2

Ingredients:
➤ 1 cup rinsed lentils

➤ 3 beetroots, cooked & cubed

➤ 2 onions, sliced

➤ 2 tablespoons hazelnuts, chopped

- A handful of parsley, chopped
- A handful of mint, chopped
- 6 tablespoons of olive oil
- ¾ inch ginger, peeled & chopped
- 1 tablespoon of apple cider vinegar
- 1 teaspoon of Dijon mustard
- 2 cups of water
- Pinch of ground black pepper and sea salt

Instructions:

1. Place the lentils in your saucepan. Cover with water and boil for 15 minutes.
2. Transfer the lentils to a bowl. Set aside for cooling.
3. Add the onions, beetroot, herbs, and hazelnuts once they are cool. Stir to combine well.
4. Put the mustard, ginger, vinegar, and oil in your bowl for the dressing.
5. Blend to combine well.
6. Drizzle dressing over your salad.

Nutrition Facts Per Serving

- *Calories 438*
- *Carbohydrates 77g*
- *Fat 2g*
- *Protein 28g*
- *Fiber 16g*
- *Sodium 1484mg*

45. Chicken & Lentil Soup with Escarole, Parsnips

Prep Time: *10 minutes/***Cook Time:** *30 minutes/***Serves:** *5*

Ingredients:

- ➤ 1 lb. parsnips
- ➤ 2 tablespoons of extra-virgin olive oil
- ➤ ½ lb. chicken breast, cooked & shredded
- ➤ ¾ cup of French lentils, rinsed
- ➤ 6 cloves of garlic, sliced
- ➤ 10 stalks of celery, sliced
- ➤ 1-1/2 cups of cooked chicken, shredded
- ➤ ½ escarole head, cut into small pieces

- ➤ 2 tablespoons of lemon juice
- ➤ ½ cup dill, chopped
- ➤ 1 teaspoon kosher salt

Instructions:

1. Keep the parsnips, chicken, lentils, and 1 teaspoon of salt in a pot.
2. Cover with 8 cups of water.
3. Boil over high temperature. Bring down the heat to medium. 10 minutes.
4. Heat oil over the medium temperature in a skillet.
5. Add the garlic and celery. Cook for 12 minutes while stirring.
6. Stir in the garlic, celery, escarole, and shredded chicken to the soup.
7. Cook for 5 minutes. Stir occasionally.
8. Remove from heat. Stir in the lemon juice and dill. Season with salt.

Nutrition Facts Per Serving

- ➤ *Calories 335*
- ➤ *Carbohydrates 40g*
- ➤ *Cholesterol 43mg*
- ➤ *Fat 10g, Fiber 16g*
- ➤ *Sugar 6g*
- ➤ *Protein 27g*
- ➤ *Sodium 561mg*

46. Lemon, Chicken & Kale Soup

Prep Time: *15 minutes/****Cook Time:*** *15 minutes/****Serves:*** *6*

Ingredients:

- ➤ 1 lb. chicken breast, boneless & skinless, cut into small pieces
- ➤ 2 tablespoons of extra-virgin olive oil
- ➤ 1 teaspoon oregano, dried
- ➤ 2 cups onions, chopped
- ➤ ¾ teaspoon pepper, ground

- 1 cup celery, chopped
- 1 cup carrots, chopped
- 1 bay leaf
- 2 garlic cloves, minced
- 2/3 cups of whole-wheat pasta
- 4 cups of chicken broth, unsalted
- 1 lemon, juiced & zested
- 4 cups of kale, chopped
- 1-1/4 teaspoon of salt

Instructions:

1. Heat a tablespoon of oil over medium temperature.
2. Add the chicken. Sprinkle oregano, pepper, and salt.
3. Cook for 4 minutes. Transfer to plate once done.
4. Add the onions, the remaining oil, celery, and carrots to your pan.
5. Cook for 4 more minutes. Add the bay leaf, the remaining oregano, and garlic.
6. Cook for a minute, while stirring.
7. Pour in the broth. Boil over high temperature.
8. Lower the heat and simmer for 5 minutes.
9. Add the chicken and kale. Keep cooking for 6 more minutes.

10.   Take out from the heat. Remove the bay leaf.

11.   Stir in the lemon juice, zest, pepper, and salt.

Nutrition Facts Per Serving

- ➢ *Calories 245*
- ➢ *Carbohydrates 24g*
- ➢ *Cholesterol 42mg*
- ➢ *Fat 8g*
- ➢ *Fiber 5g*
- ➢ *Protein 21g*
- ➢ *Sugar 5g*
- ➢ *Sodium 639mg*
- ➢ *Potassium 480mg*

47. Fennel Carrot Soup

Ingredients:

- ➤ ½ teaspoon of fennel seed
- ➤ 1 tablespoon melted coconut oil
- ➤ ½ lb. pumpkin
- ➤ 1-1/2 lb. carrots, sliced
- ➤ 1 lb. vegetable broth
- ➤ 1 apple, peeled & cubed
- ➤ 1 bay leaf
- ➤ 2 tablespoons of long-grain rice, uncooked

- ➢ 1 tablespoon of lemon juice
- ➢ ½ teaspoon of curry powder
- ➢ 2 tablespoons parsley, minced
- ➢ ¼ teaspoon of white pepper

Instructions:

1. Pour coconut oil in a saucepan. Heat over medium temperature.
2. Add fennel. Cook while stirring for 3 minutes.
3. Add the pumpkin, apple, and carrots. Cook for 5 minutes while stirring.
4. Now stir in the rice, broth, curry powder, and bay leaf. Boil.
5. Lower the heat. Cover and let it simmer for 30 minutes. The rice and vegetables should be soft.
6. Remove from heat. Set aside for cooling. Discard the bay leaf.
7. Process in your blender. Return to the pan.
8. Stir in the lemon juice, pepper, and salt.
9. Cook for 5 minutes on medium heat. Stir occasionally.
10. Sprinkle parsley and serve.

Nutrition Facts Per Serving

- ➢ Calories 110
- ➢ Carbohydrates 20g
- ➢ Cholesterol 4mg
- ➢ Fat 2g
- ➢ Fiber 4g
- ➢ Protein 2g
- ➢ Sugar 9g
- ➢ Sodium 674mg

48. Green Papaya Salad

Prep Time: *10 minutes/****Cook Time:*** *5 minutes/****Serves:*** *6*

Ingredients:

- ➢ ¼ teaspoon lime zest, grated
- ➢ ¼ cup of lime juice
- ➢ 2 tablespoons of fish sauce
- ➢ 2 tablespoons agave nectar
- ➢ 3 cups green papaya, cut
- ➢ ½ cup bean sprouts
- ➢ ½ cup onion, sliced
- ➢ Hawaiian chilies

➢ Ground pepper to taste

Instructions:

1. Whisk together the lime juice, lime zest, chilies, fish sauce, and agave in a bowl.

2. Add the onion, sprouts, and papaya to the vinaigrette. Combine well by tossing.

3. Sprinkle some pepper and serve.

Nutrition Facts Per Serving

➢ *Calories 56*

➢ *Carbohydrates 13g*

➢ *Fat 0g*

➢ *Protein 1g*

➢ *Sugar 9g*

➢ *Fiber 1g*

➢ *Sodium 403mg*

➢ *Potassium 141mg*

49. Vegan Lentil Mushroom Salad

Prep Time: *15 minutes/****Cook Time:*** *25 minutes/****Serves:*** *2*

Ingredients:

- ➢ 2 cups of vegetable stock
- ➢ ½ cup green lentils
- ➢ 4 teaspoons olive oil
- ➢ 4 cups of brown and button mushrooms
- ➢ 2 garlic cloves, chopped
- ➢ ½ onion, chopped

- 1-1/2 tablespoons of lemon juice
- ¼ teaspoon chili flakes
- 2 tablespoons of parsley, chopped
- ½ cup arugula
- Pepper and sea salt to taste

Instructions:

1. Keep the vegetable stock and lentils in your saucepan.
2. Boil and then lower to a simmer for 20 minutes. Set aside.
3. Keep your frying pan on high heat. Add a third of your mushrooms.
4. Cook for 2 minutes. Flip over and cook for 1 more minute.
5. Remove the pan. Lower the heat to medium.
6. Add 2 teaspoons of olive oil and add the onion.
7. Cook to make it golden slightly.
8. Return mushrooms to your pan. Add the chili flakes and garlic.
9. Cook for 2 minutes.
10. Now toss the mushroom, garlic, and lentils together along with the olive oil and lemon juice.
11. Add the parsley. Season to taste.

Nutrition Facts Per Serving

- ➤ Calories 194
- ➤ Carbohydrates 14g
- ➤ Fat 14g, Fiber 1g
- ➤ Protein 3g
- ➤ Sugar 5g
- ➤ Sodium 949mg
- ➤ Potassium 276mg

50. Mediterranean Spinach Tuna Salad

Prep Time: *15 minutes/****Cook Time:*** *5 minutes/****Serves:*** *1*

Ingredients:

- ➢ 1-1/2 tablespoons of lemon juice
- ➢ 1-1/2 tablespoons tahini
- ➢ 1 chunk tuna of 1/3 lb.
- ➢ 1-1/2 tablespoons of water
- ➢ 2 tablespoons of cashew paste
- ➢ 4 olives, pitted & chopped

- ➤ 2 cups of baby spinach
- ➤ 2 tablespoons of parsley, chopped
- ➤ 1 orange, peeled

Instructions:

1. Whisk together the lemon juice, water, and tahini in your bowl.
2. Add the olives, tuna, parsley, and cashew. Combine well.
3. Serve your tuna salad over two cups of spinach and orange.

Nutrition Facts Per Serving

- ➤ *Calories 442*
- ➤ *Carbohydrates 26g*
- ➤ *Cholesterol 46mg*
- ➤ *Fat 26g, Fiber 6g*
- ➤ *Protein 26g*
- ➤ *Sugar 14g*
- ➤ *Sodium 665mg*
- ➤ *Potassium 780mg*

51. Chicken Tortilla Soup

Prep Time: 20 minutes/**Cook Time:** 8 hours, 20 minutes/**Serves:** 4

Ingredients:

- ➤ 1-1/4 lb. chicken thighs, skinless, with bones
- ➤ 1 chopped onion
- ➤ ½ chopped red bell pepper
- ➤ 1 chopped garlic clove
- ➤ 2 cups chicken stock
- ➤ ¾ lb. mangoes, diced

- ➤ ½ lb. pumpkin sauce, create your own by grating and squeezing
- ➤ ¼ lb. green chili, chopped
- ➤ 1 teaspoon chili powder
- ➤ 1 teaspoon oregano, dried
- ➤ ¾ teaspoon cumin, ground
- ➤ Kosher salt to taste
- ➤ ½ teaspoon black pepper
- ➤ 2 yellow squash, sliced & halved
- ➤ 1/5 lb. green beans
- ➤ 1 tablespoon lime juice
- ➤ 2-1/2 tablespoons cilantro, chopped
- ➤ Sour cream, tortilla chips, sliced jalapeno for serving

Instructions:

1. Keep the onion, chicken, garlic, bell pepper, mangoes, stock, chili powder, pumpkin sauce, cumin and oregano in a cooker.
2. Season with pepper and salt.
3. Cover and cook for 7-8 hours on high heat.
4. Add green beans and squash.
5. Cover and cook for 30 more minutes.
6. Take out the chicken. Discard the bones. Shred the meat.

7. Keep in the slow cooker again. Stir the cilantro and lime juice in.

8. Serve with jalapeno, sour cream and cilantro.

Nutrition Facts Per Serving

- ➤ *Calories 248*
- ➤ *Cholesterol 108mg*
- ➤ *Carbohydrates 18g*
- ➤ *Fat 8g*
- ➤ *Fiber 6g*
- ➤ *Protein 26g*

52. Carrot Cucumber Salad

Ingredients:

- ➤ ¼ cup of rice vinegar, seasoned
- ➤ ½ teaspoon olive oil
- ➤ 1 teaspoon stevia
- ➤ ¼ teaspoon ginger, grated & peeled
- ➤ ¼ teaspoon salt
- ➤ 1 cup carrot, sliced
- ➤ 2 tablespoons green onion, sliced

> 2 tablespoons red bell pepper, minced
> ½ cucumber, seeded, halved, and sliced

Instructions:

1. Whisk the stevia, rice vinegar, ginger, salt, and olive oil together in your bowl.
2. Now toss the green onion, carrot, cucumber and bell pepper in this dress.
3. Coat evenly. Plastic wrap the bowl.
4. Keep in refrigerator for about 30 minutes.

Nutrition Facts Per Serving

> *Calories 57*
> *Cholesterol 0mg*
> *Carbohydrates 11g*
> *Fat 1g*
> *Fiber 2g*
> *Sugar 7g*
> *Protein 1g*

CHAPTER 10 – DESSERTS

53. Apple Cinnamon Chips

Prep Time: *5 minutes/**Cook Time:** 2 hours/**Serves:** 3*

Ingredients:

- ➢ ¾ teaspoon cinnamon, ground
- ➢ 3 large apples

Instructions:

1. Preheat your oven to 200 degrees F.
2. Line baking sheets with parchment paper.

3. Wash and core your apples. Slice them horizontally with a knife.

4. Keep them on the baking sheets in one layer. Sprinkle cinnamon.

5. Bake for an hour. Take out the baking sheets.

6. Bake for another hour.

7. Turn the oven off. Keep them in your oven for an hour to cool.

Nutrition Facts Per Serving

➢ *Calories 72*

➢ *Carbohydrates 18g*

➢ *Fiber 5g*

➢ *Sugar 11g*

➢ *Sodium 2mg*

54. Lemon Vegan Cake

Prep Time: *10 minutes/****Cook Time:*** *10 minutes/****Serves:*** *10*

Ingredients:

- ➤ 1 cup of pitted dates
- ➤ 2-1/2 cups pecans
- ➤ 1-1/2 cup agave
- ➤ 3 avocados, halved & pitted
- ➤ 3 cups of cauliflower rice, prepared
- ➤ 1 lemon juice and zest
- ➤ ½ lemon extract
- ➤ 1-1/2 cups pineapple, crushed

- ➤ 1-1/2 teaspoon vanilla extract
- ➤ Pinch of cinnamon
- ➤ 1-1/2 cups of dairy-free yogurt

Instructions:

1. Line your baking sheet with parchment paper.
2. Pulse the pecans in your food processor.
3. Add the agave and dates. Pulse for a minute.
4. Transfer this mix to the baking sheet. Wipe the bowl of your processor.
5. Bring together the pineapple, agave, avocados, cauliflower, lemon juice and zest in your food processor. Get a smooth mixture.
6. Now add the lemon extract, cinnamon, and vanilla extract. Pulse.
7. Pour this mix into your pan, on the crust.
8. Refrigerate for 5 hours minimum.
9. Take out the cake and keep it in room temperature for 20 minutes.
10. Take out the cake's outer ring.
11. Whisk together the vanilla extract, agave, and yogurt in a bowl.
12. Pour on your cake.

Nutrition Facts Per Serving

- ➤ Calories 688
- ➤ Carbohydrates 100g
- ➤ Fat 28g
- ➤ Protein 9g
- ➤ Sugar 40g

55. Dark Chocolate Granola Bars

*Prep Time: 10 minutes/**Cook Time:** 25 minutes/**Serves:** 12*

Ingredients:
- ➢ 1 cup tart cherries, dried
- ➢ 2 cups buckwheat
- ➢ ¼ cup of flaxseed
- ➢ 1 cup of walnuts
- ➢ 2 eggs
- ➢ 1 teaspoon of salt
- ➢ ¼ cup dark cocoa powder
- ➢ 2/3 cup honey

- ➤ ½ cup dark chocolate chips
- ➤ 1 teaspoon of vanilla

Instructions:

1. Preheat your oven to 350 degrees F.
2. Apply cooking spray lightly on your baking pan.
3. Pulse together the walnuts, wheat, tart cherries, salt, and flaxseed in your food processor. Everything should be chopped fine.
4. Whisk together the honey, eggs, vanilla, and cocoa powder in a bowl.
5. Add the wheat mix to your bowl. Stir to combine well.
6. Include the chocolate chips. Stir again.
7. Now pour this mixture into your baking dish.
8. Sprinkle some chocolate chips and tart cherries.
9. Bake for 25 minutes. Set aside for cooling before serving.

Nutrition Facts Per Serving

- ➤ *Calories 364*
- ➤ *Carbohydrates 37g*
- ➤ *Cholesterol 60mg*
- ➤ *Fat 20g*
- ➤ *Protein 6g*
- ➤ *Sugar 22g*
- ➤ *Fiber 4g*
- ➤ *Sodium 214mg*

56. Blueberry Crisp

Prep Time: *5 minutes/****Cook Time:*** *30 minutes/****Serves:*** *4*

Ingredients:

- ➤ ¼ cups pecans, chopped
- ➤ 1 cup buckwheat
- ➤ ½ teaspoon ginger
- ➤ 1 teaspoon of cinnamon
- ➤ 2 tablespoons olive oil
- ➤ ¼ teaspoon nutmeg
- ➤ 1 lb. blueberries
- ➤ 1 teaspoon of honey

Instructions:

1. Preheat your oven to 350 degrees F.

2. Grease your baking dish.

3. Whisk together the pecans, wheat, oil, spices, and honey in a bowl.

4. Add the berries to your pan. Layer the topping on your berries.

5. Bake for 30 minutes at 350 F.

Nutrition Facts Per Serving

- ➤ *Calories 327*
- ➤ *Carbohydrates 35g*
- ➤ *Fat 19g*
- ➤ *Protein 4g*
- ➤ *Sugar 14g*
- ➤ *Fiber 5g*
- ➤ *Sodium 2mg*
- ➤ *Potassium 197mg*

57. Chocolate Chip Quinoa Granola Bars

Prep Time: *5 minutes/****Cook Time:*** *10 minutes/****Serves:*** *16*

Ingredients:

- ➢ ½ cup of chia seeds
- ➢ ½ cup walnuts, chopped
- ➢ 1 cup buckwheat
- ➢ 1 cup uncooked quinoa
- ➢ 2/3 cup dairy-free margarine
- ➢ ½ cup flax seed

- ➢ 1 teaspoon of cinnamon
- ➢ ½ cup of honey
- ➢ ½ cup of chocolate chips
- ➢ 1 teaspoon of vanilla
- ➢ ¼ teaspoon salt

Instructions:

1. Preheat your oven to 350 degrees F.
2. Spread the walnuts, quinoa, wheat, flax, and chia on your baking sheet.
3. Bake for 10 minutes.
4. Line your baking dish with plastic wrap. Apply cooking spray. Keep aside.
5. Melt the margarine and honey in a saucepot.
6. Whisk together the vanilla, salt, and cinnamon into the margarine mix.
7. Keep the wheat mix and quinoa in a bowl. Pour the margarine sauce into it.
8. Stir the mixture. Coat well. Allow it to cool. Stir in the chocolate chips.
9. Spread your mixture into the baking dish. Press firmly into the pan.
10. Plastic wrap. Refrigerator overnight.
11. Slice into bars and serve.

Nutrition Facts Per Serving

- ➤ Calories 408
- ➤ Carbohydrates 31g
- ➤ Fat 28g
- ➤ Protein 8g
- ➤ Sugar 14g
- ➤ Fiber 6g
- ➤ Sodium 87mg

58. Strawberry Granita

Prep Time: *10 minutes*/**Cook Time:** *10 minutes*/**Serves:** *8*

Ingredients:

- ➢ 2 lb. strawberries, halved & hulled
- ➢ 1 cup of water
- ➢ Agave to taste
- ➢ ¼ teaspoon balsamic vinegar
- ➢ ½ teaspoon lemon juice
- ➢ Just a small pinch of salt

Instructions:

1. Rinse the strawberries in water.

2. Keep in a blender. Add water, agave, balsamic vinegar, salt, and lemon juice.

3. Pulse many times so that the mixture moves. Blend to make it smooth.

4. Pour into a baking dish. The puree should be 3/8 inch deep only.

5. Refrigerate the dish uncovered till the edges start to freeze. The center should be slushy.

6. Stir crystals from the edges lightly into the center. Mix thoroughly.

7. Chill till the granite is almost completely frozen.

8. Scrape loose the crystals like before and mix.

9. Refrigerate again. Use a fork to stir 3-4 times till the granite has become light.

Nutrition Facts Per Serving

➢ *Calories 72*

➢ *Carbohydrates 17g*

➢ *Fat 0g*

➢ *Sugar 14g*

➢ *Fiber 2g*

➢ *Protein 1g*

59. Apple Fritters

Prep Time: *15 minutes/****Cook Time:*** *10 minutes/****Serves:*** *4*

Ingredients:
- 1 apple, cored, peeled, and chopped
- 1 cup all-purpose flour
- 1 egg
- ½ cup cashew milk
- 1-1/2 teaspoons of baking powder
- 2 tablespoons of stevia sugar

Instructions:
1. Preheat your air fryer to 175 degrees C or 350 degrees F.

2. Keep parchment paper at the bottom of your fryer.

3. Apply cooking spray.

4. Mix together ¼ cup sugar, flour, baking powder, egg, milk, and salt in a bowl.

5. Combine well by stirring.

6. Sprinkle 2 tablespoons of sugar on the apples. Coat well.

7. Combine the apples into your flour mixture.

8. Use a cookie scoop and drop the fritters with it to the air fryer basket's bottom.

9. Now air fry for 5 minutes.

10. Flip the fritters once and fry for another 3 minutes. They should be golden.

Nutrition Facts Per Serving

- *Calories 307*
- *Carbohydrates 65g*
- *Cholesterol 48mg*
- *Total Fat 3g*
- *Protein 5g*
- *Sugar 39g*
- *Fiber 2g*
- *Sodium 248mg*

60. Roasted Bananas

Ingredients:

> ➢ 1 banana, sliced into diagonal pieces
> ➢ Avocado oil cooking spray

Instructions:

1. Take parchment paper and line the air fryer basket with it.

2. Preheat your air fryer to 190 degrees C or 375 degrees F.

3. Keep your slices of banana in the basket. They should not touch.

4. Apply avocado oil to mist the slices of banana.

5. Cook for 5 minutes.

6. Take out the basket. Flip the slices carefully.

7. Cook for 2 more minutes. The slices of banana should be caramelized and browning. Take them out from the basket.

Nutrition Facts Per Serving

- ➢ *Calories 121*
- ➢ *Carbohydrates 27g*
- ➢ *Cholesterol 0mg*
- ➢ *Total Fat 1g*
- ➢ *Protein 1g*
- ➢ *Sugar 14g*
- ➢ *Fiber 3g*
- ➢ *Sodium 1mg*

CHAPTER 11 – SIDES

61. Parmesan Roasted Broccoli

Prep Time: *10 minutes*/**Cook Time:** *20 minutes*/**Serves:** *6*

Ingredients:

- ➢ 3 tablespoons of olive oil
- ➢ 4 cups of broccoli florets
- ➢ 3 tablespoons of vegan parmesan, grated
- ➢ ½ teaspoon of Italian seasoning
- ➢ 1 tablespoon of lemon juice
- ➢ 1 tablespoon parsley, chopped

➢ Pepper and salt to taste

Instructions:

1. Preheat your oven to 450 degrees F. Apply cooking spray on your pan.

2. Keep the broccoli florets in a freezer bag.

3. Now add the Italian seasoning, olive oil, pepper, and salt.

4. Seal your bag. Shake it. Coat well.

5. Pour your broccoli on the pan. It should be in one layer.

6. Bake for 20 minutes. Stir halfway through.

7. Take out from your oven. Sprinkle parsley and parmesan.

8. Drizzle some lemon juice.

9. You can garnish with lemon wedges if you want.

Nutrition Facts Per Serving

➢ *Calories 96*

➢ *Carbohydrates 4g*

➢ *Cholesterol 2mg*

➢ *Total Fat 8g*

➢ *Protein 2g*

➢ *Sugar 1g*

➢ *Fiber 1g*

➢ *Sodium 58mg*

➢ *Potassium 191mg*

62. Thyme with Honey-Roasted Carrots

Prep Time: *5 minutes/****Cook Time:*** *30 minutes/****Serves:*** *4*

Ingredients:

- ➤ 1/5 lb. carrots, with the tops
- ➤ 1 tablespoon of honey
- ➤ 2 tablespoons of olive oil
- ➤ ½ teaspoon thyme, dried
- ➤ ½ teaspoon of sea salt

Instructions:

1. Preheat your oven to 425 degrees F.

2. Keep parchment paper on your baking sheet.

3. Toss your carrots with honey, oil, thyme, and salt. Coat well.

4. Keep in a single layer. Bake in your oven for 30 minutes.

5. Set aside for cooling before serving.

Nutrition Facts Per Serving

➢ *Calories 85*

➢ *Carbohydrates 6g*

➢ *Cholesterol 0mg*

➢ *Total Fat 8g*

➢ *Protein 1g*

➢ *Sugar 6g*

➢ *Fiber 1g*

➢ *Sodium 244mg*

63. Roasted Parsnips

Prep Time: *5 minutes/****Cook Time:*** *30 minutes/****Serves:*** *4*

Ingredients:

- ➢ 1 tablespoon of extra-virgin olive oil
- ➢ 2 lbs. parsnips
- ➢ 1 teaspoon of kosher salt
- ➢ 1-1/2 teaspoon of Italian seasoning
- ➢ Chopped parsley for garnishing

Instructions:

1. Preheat your oven to 400 degrees F.

2. Peel the parsnips. Cut them into one-inch chunks.

3. Now toss with the seasoning, salt, and oil in a bowl.

4. Spread this on your baking sheet. It should be in one layer.

5. Roast for 30 minutes. Stir every ten minutes.

6. Transfer to a plate. Garnish with parsley.

Nutrition Facts Per Serving

- ➢ *Calories 124*
- ➢ *Carbohydrates 20g*
- ➢ *Total Fat 4g*
- ➢ *Protein 2g*
- ➢ *Fiber 4g*
- ➢ *Sugar 5g*
- ➢ *Sodium 550mg*

64. Green Beans

Prep Time: *5 minutes/****Cook Time:*** *10 minutes/****Serves:*** *5*

Ingredients:

- ➤ ½ teaspoon of red pepper flakes
- ➤ 2 tablespoons of extra-virgin olive oil
- ➤ 2 garlic cloves, minced
- ➤ 1-1/2 lbs. green beans, trimmed
- ➤ 2 tablespoons of water
- ➤ ½ teaspoon kosher salt

Instructions:

1. Heat oil in a skillet over medium temperature.

2. Include the pepper flake. Stir to coat in the olive oil.

3. Include the green beans. Cook for 7 minutes.

4. Stir often. The beans should be brown in some areas.

5. Add the salt and garlic. Cook for 1 minute, while stirring.

6. Pour water and cover immediately.

7. Cook covered for 1 more minute.

Nutrition Facts Per Serving

- ➢ *Calories 82*
- ➢ *Carbohydrates 6g*
- ➢ *Total Fat 6g*
- ➢ *Protein 1g*
- ➢ *Fiber 2g*
- ➢ *Sugar 0g*
- ➢ *Sodium 230mg*

65. Roasted Carrots

Ingredients:

- ➤ 1 onion, peeled & cut
- ➤ 8 carrots, peeled & cut
- ➤ 1 teaspoon thyme, chopped
- ➤ 2 tablespoons of extra-virgin olive oil
- ➤ ½ teaspoon rosemary, chopped
- ➤ ¼ teaspoon ground pepper
- ➤ ½ teaspoon salt

Instructions:

1. Preheat your oven to 425 degrees F.

2. Mix the onions and carrots by tossing in a bowl with rosemary, thyme, pepper, and salt. Spread on your baking sheet.

3. Roast for 40 minutes. The onions and carrots should be browning and tender.

Nutrition Facts Per Serving

- *Calories 126*
- *Carbohydrates 16g*
- *Total Fat 6g*
- *Protein 2g*
- *Fiber 4g*
- *Sugar 8g*
- *Sodium 286mg*

CHAPTER 12 – BEVERAGE AND BROTHS

66. Turmeric and Apple Cider Vinegar Detox Tea

Prep Time: 5 minutes/**Cook Time:** 5 minutes/**Serves:** 2

Ingredients:

> ½ teaspoon turmeric powder, ground
>
> 2 bags of green tea

- ➢ 2 cups of hot water
- ➢ 2 tablespoons of honey
- ➢ 2 tablespoons of apple cider vinegar
- ➢ Slices of lemon to garnish

Instructions:

1. Add the tea bags to glasses. Pour boiling water into them.
2. Set aside for 5 minutes.
3. Add equal portions of the turmeric powder into both the glasses.
4. Pour a teaspoon of honey and Apple Cider Vinegar into each glass.
5. Mix well by stirring.
6. Garnish with lemon slices.

Nutrition Facts Per Serving

- ➢ *Calories 94*
- ➢ *Carbohydrates 18g*
- ➢ *Total Fat 2g*
- ➢ *Protein 1g*
- ➢ *Sugar 17g*
- ➢ *Sodium 14mg*

67. Lemon Drop Mocktail

Prep Time: *5 minutes/****Cook Time:*** *2 minutes/****Serves:*** *1*

Ingredients:

- ➢ 2 tablespoons of lemon juice
- ➢ 4 tablespoons of carbonated water, chilled
- ➢ 1-1/2 tablespoons of maple syrup
- ➢ 1 teaspoon stevia sugar and ice

Instructions:

1. Keep your stevia on a plate.
2. Wet the rim of a glass with water or half of the lemon.

3. Now dip your glass rim into the stevia. Coat around the rim.

4. Shake the syrup, lemon juice, and ice cubes for 15 seconds.

5. Strain this mix into your glass.

6. Top with carbonated water.

7. You can garnish with the lemon peel.

Nutrition Facts Per Serving

➤ *Calories 101*
➤ *Carbohydrates 23g*
➤ *Cholesterol 0mg*
➤ *Total Fat 1g*
➤ *Sugar 5g*
➤ *Sodium 39mg*

68. Celery Juice

Prep Time: *2 minutes/****Cook Time:*** *5 minutes/****Serves:*** *1*

Ingredients:

> ➢ 1.5 lbs. organic celery
> ➢ 1 cup of water

Instructions:

1. Wash and rinse your celery in cold water.

2. Peel and trim the brown parts and leaves. Slice into small pieces.

3. Keep the celery in a blender. Blend in smoothie mode.

4. Use a strainer to strain its pulp.

Nutrition Facts Per Serving

- ➤ *Calories 109*
- ➤ *Carbohydrates 20g*
- ➤ *Total Fat 1g*
- ➤ *Fiber 11g*
- ➤ *Sugar 12g*
- ➤ *Protein 5g*
- ➤ *Sodium 556mg*
- ➤ *Potassium 1769mg*

69. Strawberry Green Tea

Ingredients:

- ➤ 4 bags of green tea
- ➤ ½ cup of black tapioca pearls
- ➤ 4 cups of water
- ➤ ¼ lb. strawberry, sliced
- ➤ ½ cup honey
- ➤ 2 cups of ice cubes

Instructions:

1. Prepare your tapioca pearls. Keep them immersed in water.

2. Make your tea in a pitcher. Add hot water to your teabags.

3. Now add the honey. Stir well.

4. Keep it refrigerated for an hour.

5. Take out and add the ice cubes and strawberry. Mix well.

Nutrition Facts Per Serving

- ➢ *Calories 140*
- ➢ *Carbohydrates 35g*
- ➢ *Sugar 24g*
- ➢ *Sodium 10mg*
- ➢ *Potassium 43mg*

70. Raspberry Lemonade

Prep Time: 5 minutes/Cook Time: 5 minutes/Serves: 6

Ingredients:

- 6 cups of coconut water
- 1/3 lb. raspberries
- 5 tablespoons of agave nectar
- 5 tablespoons of lemon juice
- 2 cups of ice
- Lemon wedges to garnish

Instructions:

1. Rinse and drain the raspberries. Keep them in a blender. Puree.

2. Bring together the coconut water, raspberry, agave, and lemon juice in a pitcher. Mix well.

3. Add ice to your pitcher.

4. Pour your raspberry lemonade into glasses.

5. Use lemon wedges for garnishing.

Nutrition Facts Per Serving

> ➢ *Calories 759*
> ➢ *Carbohydrates 26g*
> ➢ *Total Fat 71g*
> ➢ *Sugar 18g*
> ➢ *Protein 4g*
> ➢ *Fiber 5g*
> ➢ *Sodium 25mg*
> ➢ *Potassium 476mg*

CHAPTER 13 – SAUCES AND DRESSING

71. Turmeric Tahini Dressing

Prep Time: *10 minutes/****Cook Time:*** *3 minutes/****Serves:*** *8*

Ingredients:

- ¼ cup of lemon juice
- ¼ cup of tahini
- 1 tablespoon extra-virgin olive oil
- 2 tablespoons of water

- ➢ ½ tablespoon maple syrup
- ➢ 1 tablespoon of nutritional yeast
- ➢ ¼ teaspoon turmeric, ground
- ➢ 1/8 teaspoon of cayenne pepper
- ➢ ¼ teaspoon of pepper and sea salt

Instructions:

1. Add everything into a bowl. Whisk together to make it smooth.
2. Add some water if the dressing appears too thick.

Nutrition Facts Per Serving

- ➢ *Calories 87*
- ➢ *Carbohydrates 4g*
- ➢ *Total Fat 7g*
- ➢ *Sugar 1g*
- ➢ *Protein 2g*
- ➢ *Fiber 1g*
- ➢ *Sodium 56mg*

72. Anti-Inflammatory Salad Dressing

Prep Time: *10 minutes/****Cook Time:*** *3 minutes/****Serves:*** *4*

Ingredients:

- ➢ 1 tablespoon of chia seeds
- ➢ ¼ cup of raw cherries
- ➢ 1 tablespoon of apple cider vinegar
- ➢ 2/3 cup dairy-free cashew milk
- ➢ ½ teaspoon turmeric, ground
- ➢ ½ teaspoon ginger, minced

- ➢ 1 tablespoon of raw honey
- ➢ 1/8 teaspoon of mustard powder
- ➢ ½ teaspoon curry powder
- ➢ 1/8 teaspoon of black pepper and salt

Instructions:

1. Keep the chia seeds and milk in a food processor. Grind and mix.
2. Place this mix in your blender. Add some more cashew milk.
3. Blend for a minute.
4. Now add the vinegar, honey, ginger, turmeric, curry, pepper, salt, and mustard.
5. Puree for a minute. Adjust the seasoning if needed.
6. Refrigerate for half an hour.
7. Whisk or blend before pouring on your salad.

Nutrition Facts Per Serving
- ➢ *Calories 81*
- ➢ *Carbohydrates 8g*
- ➢ *Total Fat 5g*
- ➢ *Cholesterol 0mg*
- ➢ *Sugar 5g*
- ➢ *Protein 1g*
- ➢ *Sodium 2mg*

73. Ginger & Turmeric Dressing

Prep Time: *5 minutes/****Cook Time:*** *5 minutes/****Serves:*** *10*

Ingredients:

- ➢ 2 teaspoons ginger, skin removed
- ➢ 1/5 lb. of lemon juice
- ➢ 2 teaspoon turmeric, ground
- ➢ 1 clove of garlic
- ➢ 3 tablespoons of extra-virgin olive oil
- ➢ 1 teaspoon of honey

- ➢ 1 tablespoon of apple cider vinegar
- ➢ Black pepper and Himalayan salt to taste

Instructions:

1. Keep all the ingredients in your blender.
2. Mix to combine well.
3. Adjust the seasoning if needed.
4. Pour over roasted vegetables or salad.

Nutrition Facts Per Serving

- ➢ *Calories 61*
- ➢ *Carbohydrates 3g*
- ➢ *Cholesterol 0mg*
- ➢ *Fat 7g*
- ➢ *Sugar 1g*
- ➢ *Protein 1g*
- ➢ *Fiber 1g*
- ➢ *Sodium 1mg*

74. Strawberry Sauce

Prep Time: *5 minutes/**Cook Time:*** *25 minutes/**Serves:*** *2*

Ingredients:

- ➤ 1 lb. strawberries, hulled & sliced
- ➤ ½ juiced lemon
- ➤ ¼ cup of agave nectar
- ➤ ¼ cup of water

Instructions:

1. Combine everything in a pot over medium heat.
2. Boil and cook for 25 minutes over medium heat.

Nutrition Facts Per Serving

- *Calories 189*
- *Carbohydrates 43g*
- *Cholesterol 0mg*
- *Fat 1g*
- *Sugar 37g*
- *Protein 2g*
- *Fiber 5g*
- *Sodium 3mg*

75. Coriander Chutney

Prep Time: *5 minutes/****Cook Time:*** *10 minutes/****Serves:*** *2*

Ingredients:

- ½ inch ginger, chopped
- 1 cup coriander leaves, chopped
- 1 teaspoon of lemon juice
- 1 green chili, chopped
- ½ teaspoon of cumin powder
- Sea salt to taste

Instructions:

1. Add a cup of coriander leaves, ginger, and the green chili in your blender.

2. Include a teaspoon of lemon juice, salt, and cumin powder.

3. Blend everything until it turns smooth.

4. Check your seasoning. Add more lemon juice or salt if needed.

Nutrition Facts Per Serving

➢ *Calories 20*

➢ *Carbohydrates 5g*

➢ *Sugar 1g*

➢ *Fiber 1g*

➢ *Sodium 1322mg*

➢ *Potassium 83mg*

PART THREE: 2-WEEK MEAL PLAN

The human body has a defense mechanism, which prevents us from falling ill immediately. This is why it will try to fight a virus attack or some other problem. We fall ill only after this defense falls after repeated attacks or a chronic attack.

Similarly, there is hardly any magic solution. It takes time to rectify a problem. However, having said this, you can still see a quick improvement, if you begin eating the right foods, and follow the right lifestyle.

Here is a 2-weeks meal plan, which will set you in the right direction. By the end of the 2nd week, you will see a definite improvement in your inflammatory symptoms.

CHAPTER 14 – WEEK 1

Day 1

Meal	Calories
Breakfast - Quinoa and Black Beans	162
Lunch - Grilled Avocado Sandwich	340
Snacks - Spicy Kale Chips	34
Dinner - Chicken with Herb Parmesan Spaghetti Squash	295

Notes

_____
_____
_____
_____

Day 2

Meal	Calories
Breakfast - Banana Bread	240
Lunch - Grilled Salmon Burgers	395
Snacks - Lemony Quinoa	117
Dinner - Chicken Lemon Piccata	227

Notes

_____
_____
_____
_____

Day 3

Meal	Calories
Breakfast - Baked Apples	64
Lunch - Chicken Marsala	546
Snacks - Green Papaya Salad	56
Dinner - Zucchini and Lemon Herb Salmon	355

Notes

_____

_____

_____

Day 4

Meal	Calories
Breakfast - Pumpkin Pancakes	165
Lunch - Mushroom Farro Risotto	397
Snacks - White Beans with Pepper	154
Dinner - Italian Stuffed Peppers	276

Notes

_____

_____

_____

Day 5

Meal	Calories
Breakfast - Mashed Cauliflower	64
Lunch - Rosemary Garlic Lamb Chops	678
Snacks - 1/2 Cup Blueberries	42
Dinner - Italian Stuffed Peppers	276

Notes

_____
_____
_____
_____

Day 6

Meal	Calories
Breakfast - Cinnamon Raisin Bread	207
Lunch - Air Fryer Salmon	305
Snacks - Cauliflower Popcorn	121
Dinner - Lemon, Chicken & Kale Soup	245

Notes

_____
_____
_____
_____

Day 7

Meal	Calories
Breakfast - Protein Pancakes	106
Lunch - Tuna Steaks	141
Snacks - 12 Walnut Halves	157
Dinner - Parmesan and Lemon Fish	191

Notes

_____
_____
_____
_____

CHAPTER 15 – WEEK 2

Day 8

Meal	Calories
Breakfast - Whole Grain Blueberry Scones	331
Lunch - Turkey Burgers	316
Snacks - 15 Unsalted Almonds	116
Dinner - Chicken Marrakesh	520

Notes

_____
_____
_____
_____

Day 9

Meal	Calories
Breakfast - Lemon Avocado Toast	69
Lunch - Cauliflower Steaks with Tamarind and Beans	1366
Snacks - 1/2 Cup Sliced Cucumber	9
Dinner - Vegetable and Chicken Stir Fry	183

Notes

_____
_____
_____
_____

Day 10

Meal	Calories
Breakfast - Baked French Toast Casserole	200
Lunch - Instant Pot Black Beans	144
Snacks - Blueberry-Lemon Bread	200
Dinner - Toasted Brown Rice with Thyme and Mushrooms	62

Notes

_____

_____

_____

_____

Day 11

Meal	Calories
Breakfast - Zucchini Noodle Breakfast Bowl	362
Lunch - Popcorn Chicken	156
Snacks - Cacao Coffee Protein Bars	280
Dinner - Shrimp and Vegetable Curry	491

Notes

_____

_____

_____

_____

Day 12

Meal	Calories
Breakfast - Thyme with Honey-Roasted Carrots	85
Lunch - Avocado and Shrimp Lettuce Wraps	256
Snacks - Vegan Lentil Mushroom Salad	194
Dinner - Baked Tilapia with Rosemary and Pecan	244

Notes

_____

_____

_____

_____

Day 13

Meal	Calories
Breakfast - Raspberry Power Smoothie	249
Lunch - Vegan Superfood Bowl	381
Snacks - 2/3 Cup Raspberries	42
Dinner - Blackened Chicken Breast	424

Notes

_____

_____

_____

_____

Day 14

Meal	Calories
Breakfast - Broccoli-Turkey Brunch Casserole	299
Lunch - Smoked Salmon Tartine	734
Snacks - Spicy Tuna Rolls	129
Dinner - Fennel Carrot Soup	110

Notes

_____

_____

_____

_____

PART FOUR: TIPS FOR AN ANTI-INFLAMMATORY DIET

Here are some tips that will surely help you –

1. **Reduce the intake of sugar** – The added sugar many of us consume is never good for health. There is enough evidence that proves that sugar triggers inflammatory diseases. So stop having anything where there are artificial sweeteners or added sugars for a week. Read the food labels carefully. Drink your tea or coffee without sugar. You will see a marked improvement.

2. **Eat fewer calories** – It is well known by now that people who eat a low-calorie diet suffer from fewer diseases and live longer. One key reason for this is because they don't suffer from chronic inflammation. Even a 30% to 40% reduction is going to help you. Start slowly, like 10%, for instance, because there can be health concerns if you make severe restrictions suddenly. Scale-up gradually. Replace with healthy fats and complex carbohydrates.

3. **Eat complex carbohydrates** – Most of the carbs you get should be from non-starchy vegetables, such as

chickpeas, beans, lentils, and 100% whole-grain rice and bread. It will be even better if you can focus on legumes and veggies instead of rice and grains. Take fewer simple carbs like refined rice, grains, sugar, and starchy vegetables, such as corn and potatoes.

4. **Starches** – Limit the intake of refined starches. These foods are not as nutrient-dense and can promote the symptoms of inflammation like increasing the level of blood glucose, enhancing the lipid levels, and promoting weight gain. Whole-grain starches are nutrient-dense and provide a lot of minerals and vitamins that will help you improve your health and maintain it.

5. **Vital nutrients** – Eat fish, skinless poultry, fat-free Greek yogurt, eggs, and legumes. They are all a good source of protein. You will also get a lot of vitamin D, calcium, unsaturated fat, and probiotics.

6. **Red meat** – Also remember to eat high-fat red meat with moderation. So go easy on your sausage, bacon, prime rib, and also processed meats, such as salami, hot dogs, and bologna. They have a lot more saturated fats that will certainly increase inflammation.

7. **Fish, Seafood** – It will be great if you can have two to three servings in a week. Pick from sardines, salmon, anchovies, cod, clams, shrimp, trout, and sea bream. You can get more anti-inflammatory omega-3 fats from these species. People from the Mediterranean region eat a lot of these fishes. It has been observed that they suffer fewer ailments and live longer. High mercury content fish like tuna, halibut, mackerel, and swordfish should be limited to one serving.

8. **Go vegetarian** – At least semi-vegetarian if you cannot live without non-veg food. Try to eat vegetarian food two times a week. Animal proteins have been linked to a higher risk of inflammation. Evidence also suggests that there are fewer cases of vegans and vegetarians that suffer from heart disease and inflammation.

9. **Veggies and fruits** – The V's and F's are rich in vitamins, antioxidants, and minerals. Make sure that you eat colorful veggies and fruits. Keep it interesting by picking something different every week. Citrus fruits, strawberries, kiwis, broccoli, Brussels sprouts, sweet potatoes, tomatoes, sweet bell peppers, carrots, and spinach all provide antioxidants that can reduce inflammation.

10. **Fats** – Limit the saturated fats you get from whole milk, butter, high-fat red meat, cheese, and poultry with skin. The human body only needs a small quantity of these fats. There will be an inflammatory response if you keep adding excess amounts every day. Also, avoid trans fats completely. You find them in flavored coffee creams, pre-packaged baked products, yogurt or chocolate-coated snacks, peanut butter from the shelf and other products. You cannot have trans fats safely, even in small quantities. The bad cholesterol level in your body is bound to go up.

11. **The cooking oil** – Olive oil should be the main oil you use for cooking, and also for your salad dressings. It's best to avoid vegetable oils, such as corn oil and soybean that you will find in pre-made packaged foods.

12. **Healthy weight** – You will have a higher risk of chronic inflammation and its related diseases if you are obese or overweight. Several studies have established this as a fact. So make every effort to shed those excess pounds. Get adequate exercise. Make some lifestyle changes.

13. **Alcohol consumption** – Drinking too much alcohol can also increase inflammation. So limit the intake. Women should restrict themselves to just 1 drink daily, and men to 2. Say no to beer. You can drink red wine, but with limitations. Always read the added sugar content in the label of your alcohol.

14. **Gut bacteria** – Studies have revealed that a disturbed microbiome can cause chronic inflammation and eventually inflammatory disorders.

15. **Omega-3** – These fatty acids are good for health. They can neutralize inflammation efficiently. You will get them from ground flaxseed, walnuts, tuna, and wild-caught salmon. The human body cannot make omega-3, but they are essential for us. Thus, we have to get them from supplements or dietary sources. It is always better to get your omega-3 from natural sources.

CHAPTER 16 – TOP 15 ANTI-INFLAMMATORY SUPER FOODS

Eating the right foods can make a world of difference. So be careful about what you have in your meals. However, having said this, here are some superfoods that are always going to be good for you, no matter what your age or health condition is.

1. **Berries** – There are plenty of varieties. The most common ones include blueberries, strawberries, blackberries, and raspberries. They come loaded with minerals, vitamins, and fiber. Berries have the anthocyanins antioxidants, which are compounds with **anti-inflammatory effects** (21).

   In a study, researchers found that people who ate berries daily produced a higher number of NK cells that help the immune system function properly. A second study discovered that obese adults were able to lower some inflammatory markers related to heart disease by eating strawberries.

2. **Avocado** – This fruit has a lot of monounsaturated fats and vitamin E, two key anti-inflammatory powerhouses, which will keep your skin healthy, improve brain function, and help you stay away from joint pains. It even promotes cardiovascular health.

An avocado will give you fiber, potassium, and magnesium. It has a low sodium content. Just half an avocado will give you adequate vitamins A, C, B-complex and E for a day. These nutrients and polyphenols, which are antioxidants, make this fruit a powerful anti-inflammatory **superfood** (22).

3. **Salmon** – There are few better nutrients than omega-3 fatty acids. Wild-caught salmon is especially good as this fish will give you a lot of omega-3. In fact, you will get more of these fatty acids from salmon than from any other fish.

Studies have revealed that people who consume more fatty acids have a healthier heart. Healthy fats also keep cholesterol under check and reduce inflammation. Another study found that there was a **reduction** (23) in C-reactive protein, an inflammatory marker, among those who ate salmon.

The American Heart Association has recommended that we eat fatty fish like salmon two times a week.

4. **Broccoli** – Broccoli, like kale, Brussels sprouts, and cauliflower, is a cruciferous vegetable. It is extremely nutritious. Cruciferous veggies can **lower** (24) the risk of cancer and heart disease as per epidemiological studies. This could be because of their antioxidant content and anti-inflammatory effects.

   The antioxidant sulforaphane in broccoli fights inflammation by lowering the NF-Kb and cytokine levels that can drive up inflammation. Furthermore, broccoli will also provide you with calcium, potassium, and vitamins A and C.

5. **Cherries** – Cherries have anthocyanins which are the nutrient that makes them dark in color. Anthocyanins have anti-inflammatory properties. They also have the catechin antioxidant that fights inflammation. You can have cherries raw or make a smoothie.

   A study found that those who ate 280 grams of cherries in a day for a month were able to keep their CRP inflammatory marker low for up to 28 days. The marker stayed low even after they stopped having cherries.

6. **Bell Peppers** – These peppers and such other brightly colored fruits and vegetables have a lot of antioxidant nutrients. They will also give you fiber, minerals, and vitamins. Bell peppers are a very good source of potassium, and vitamins A and C.

   Recent **research** (25) has also informed us that bell peppers activate thermogenesis or heat production within us, which increases the metabolic rate without increasing the blood pressure or heart rate. So a diet of bell peppers will also help you lose weight.

7. **Olive Oil** – Olive oil gives you one of the best anti-inflammatory fats. Plus, it will also lower the LDL bad cholesterol in your body. This is a star ingredient along with omega-3-rich fish.

   It will reduce inflammation and high cholesterol. It has a lot of monounsaturated fats, which are good for the blood vessels. Olive oils also have polyphenols that protect our cells and **prevent** (26) cancer.

So use olive oil in your cooking and salad dressings. It is an essential part of the Mediterranean diet. It has been seen that people from Mediterranean countries live longer and have fewer ailments.

8. **Pineapple** – This is also an anti-inflammatory superfood because of the presence of the bromelain enzyme. Bromelain improves protein digestion within us. Loaded with nutrients, pineapples speed up recovery after surgery, improves the symptoms of arthritis, boosts immunity, and even lowers the risk of some types of cancer.

You can have them raw or prepare juice. This tangy fruit is very satisfying.

9. **Green Tea** – Rarely will you find a healthier beverage. Green tea will bring down the **risk** (27) of Alzheimer's disease, cancer, and heart disease. It will also help you lose weight.

Many of the benefits of green tea come from its anti-inflammatory and antioxidant properties, particularly from the EGCG or epigallocatechin-3-gallate substance. EGCG lowers the production of proinflammatory cytokine that damages our cells, thus obstructing inflammation.

10. **Carrots** – This root vegetable is also very good for your health. Carrots have beta-carotene, which the body converts into vitamin A. They have carotenoids lutein and zeaxanthin, which too helps you with vitamin A. This low-calorie food may even **protect** (28) you against cancer according to the results of some studies.

You can have a lot of these powerful antioxidants without a worry. Eat carrots in your meals. Have them as snacks. A carrot diet will help you lose weight too.

11. **Turmeric** – This spice has an earthy strong flavor. Popular in India, it is used to make curries. Turmeric is very good for your health because of the potent anti-inflammatory nutrient curcumin. It brings down inflammation related to **diabetes** (29), arthritis, and some other diseases.

Just a gram taken daily combined with piperine that you will find in black pepper can lower the CRP inflammatory marker in people suffering from the metabolic syndrome. Piperine improves the absorption of curcumin. You don't need a lot of turmeric in your foods.

12. **Mushrooms** – There are thousands of varieties of mushrooms, but we can eat only a few of them like shiitake, truffles, and Portobello mushrooms. These low-calorie foods have a lot of vitamin B, copper, and selenium.

Mushrooms also have phenols and antioxidants that will provide you with anti-inflammatory **protection** (30). Lion's mane mushrooms are known to prevent dementia, provide relief from anxiety and depression, helps us recover from nervous system injuries, and reduces the risk of heart disease.

13. **Walnuts** – This omega-3-rich anti-inflammatory snack is a top superfood. Only a handful of these unsalted and raw walnuts will help you lower the level of LDL cholesterol and blood pressure. They will also enhance brain health.

Seeds and nuts like walnuts give you the healthy omega-3 alpha-linolenic acid. Most foods we have are rich in omega-6 fatty acids, while we end up with very little omega-3. There can be chronic inflammation if the ratio of omega-3 and omega-6 is out of balance.

Walnuts are a great source of plant-based omega-3, so prepare recipes with these seeds. You can also have them as a snack.

14. **Beans** – Beans are low in fat and provide a lot of fiber that lowers cholesterol and reduces inflammation. You will always have plenty of options as there are so many varieties of beans. Eat kidney beans, navy beans, black beans, and pinto beans. You will get B-complex vitamins, minerals, proteins, and vitamin K. The polyphenols in them work as an **antioxidant** (31).

Rich in proteins, beans are a good replacement for meat. Scientific studies have revealed that they may prevent high blood pressure, diabetes, and heart disease.

15. **Grapes** – Grapes have anthocyanins that have anti-inflammatory properties. They also have the resveratrol compound, which provides various

health benefits. You will have a significantly lower risk of diabetes, heart **disease** (32), eye disorders, obesity, and Alzheimer's if you consume grapes.

In a study, people with heart disease were asked to consume grapes extract. It was seen that there was a decrease in the inflammatory gene markers like NF-kB. The adiponectin level also increased. Low level of the adiponectin hormone promotes weight gain.

CHAPTER 17 – ANTI-INFLAMMATORY DIET AND INTERMITTENT FASTING. HOW TO COMBINE THE TWO

Medical doctors and researchers have been telling us for quite some time to eat less during meals. Spread out your food intake throughout the day, but reduce the portion sizes during each meal. It now appears that intermittent fasting could also be good for health, especially to overcome inflammation.

What is Intermittent Fasting?

Also called IF, this is a fasting technique where you don't eat for 12 to 16 hours a day. You are only allowed to have low-calorie beverages and water during this time. You need to follow this routine for a couple of times a week.

You can skip a meal, or you may want to limit your intake instead of complete fasting. The second option could be better for those who face problems in not eating for a period of 12 or more hours.

Intermittent fasting can be difficult, especially if you have just started or if you jump into this too quickly. It can be particularly difficult for women as there can be negative hormonal effects, mood changes, and the menstrual cycle can also change. But done efficiently, IF can help even women.

A modified fasting plan may work better, where you fast 2 days in a week, but these days should not be consecutive. Say, for example, you fast on Tuesday and Friday. This will ensure that your hormonal balance does not go for a toss.

It works like this...

> Fast for 2-3 non-consecutive days (Monday, Wednesday, and Friday)
> Start with 2 days a week. Add a third day once you feel comfortable.
> Practice yoga on your fasting days. Do some light cardio or strength training.
> Don't eat for 12-16 hours.
> Make sure you have enough water. You can also have tea, coffee, or juice. But make sure not to add sweeteners or milk.
> Have a normal eating schedule on the other days of the week.

Start with 12 hours, twice a week. See whether hunger is driving you mad and whether you have enough stamina and energy left in your body. Take a break if it is too much for you. Extend it to 16 hours once you are comfortable and then add a third day.

Does Intermittent Fasting Work

According to the **findings** (33) of a new study, intermittent fasting can reduce inflammation. It found that IF reduces the number of monocyte cells in the blood that can cause inflammatory symptoms.

Dr Miriam Merad from New York's Icahn School of Medicine feels people are overeating in the western world, and this is affecting the number of inflammation-causing cells we have in our body. We can do with fewer of these monocyte cells.

Kristin Kirkpatrick from the Cleveland Clinic Wellness Institute agrees. Kristin says we are over-fueling all the time, and this is opening up the inflammatory pathways. Time-restricted eating will limit that, she adds.

What the Researchers Found

The participants in this study were not allowed to eat from noon to 3 PM, and then again between 8 in the evening to 3 PM of the next day. They could only have water.

Blood samples were taken at 3 PM on both the days to find the level of white blood cells in the body. WBCs (monocytes are a type) protect against infection and show whether there is inflammation. It was seen that the monocyte level dropped sharply.

A **study** (34) carried out in 2013 arrived at the same conclusion. It concluded by noting that fasting can reduce inflammation by lowering oxidative stress in the cells. A third study carried out a year later **discovered** (35) that both alternate-day and intermittent fasting were effective in reducing insulin resistance.

Benefits of Intermittent Fasting

Periods of fasting can provide several anti-inflammatory responses –

> ➢ You will see a positive change in the overall gut microbiota composition

- Better immune response in your cells
- Insulin resistance will go down, lowering the risk of diabetes
- There will be a reduction in the inflammatory markers like C-reactive protein and cytokines
- Lower production of the β- hydroxybutyrate compound that blocks the immune system, causing inflammatory problems like Alzheimer's disease, rheumatoid arthritis, and diabetes.

There are many health gains of intermittent fasting. The process can give your human growth hormones a boost, allow cell repair, promote muscle gain, help you lose belly fat, provide more energy, improve the blood cholesterol level, allow more mental clarity, and even reverse type-2 diabetes.

CHAPTER 18 – FOODS THAT INCREASE INFLAMMATION

Certain foods are known to increase the level of inflammatory chemicals in the body. Like omega-6 fatty **acids** (36). But remember, omega-3 fatty acids are good for health because they promote the function of your brain, helps us maintain bone health, and also regulates our metabolism.

So we shouldn't remove them completely from our diet. You have to balance the consumption of omega-6 and omega-3 to stay away from chronic inflammation.

Foods that have a lot of omega-6 fatty acids include,

➢ Dairy products like cheese, milk, ice cream, and butter
➢ Meat
➢ Margarine
➢ Vegetable oils like safflower, corn, peanut, and cottonseed oil. Stop taking vegetable oils. Go for avocado oil or olive oil instead.

Sugary and processed foods – Foods you shouldn't eat includes anything overly greasy, highly processed, or extremely sweet. Studies have **shown** (37) that consumption of high-glycemic-index foods, such as refined grains and sugar that you will find in many processed foods and white bread will increase inflammation. So completely avoid or limit the consumption of refined carbohydrates, sugary drinks, processed snacks, and desserts.

Gluten – There are inflammatory reactions in some people when they have gluten. Glutens are a group of proteins, known as glutelins and prolamins. However, not everyone can have a gluten-free diet. It is also restrictive. But, if you believe that gluten could be triggering your symptoms, then it is best to try and eliminate it for some time and see whether the symptoms go away.

Nightshades – There are some plants from the family of nightshade like eggplants, tomatoes, potatoes, and peppers that also seem to trigger inflammatory conditions in some people, even though the scientific community has not yet confirmed this. However, it still might be a good idea to stay away from them for a couple of weeks to see whether the symptoms are improving.

Carbohydrates – There is **evidence** (38), though, that a high carbohydrate diet can increase inflammation, even if the carbs you have are healthy. But, many carb-rich foods like whole grains and sweet potatoes are very good, because they give you antioxidants and many vital nutrients the body requires.

So the foods you should avoid or limit are –

- ➤ Processed snacks like crackers and chips
- ➤ Foods with added salt or sugar
- ➤ Premade desserts like candy, ice cream, and cookies
- ➤ Processed carbohydrates you get in white pasta, white bread, baked goods
- ➤ Unhealthy oils
- ➤ Whole milk, cheese, and butter because of their saturated fat. Opt for low-fat dairy products instead.
- ➤ Processed red meat, such as hot dogs because they are rich in saturated fat
- ➤ Fried chicken, French fries, and other fried foods. They are not healthy even if you cook them using extra-virgin olive oil. Safflower and corn have omega-6 fatty acids. But if you have too much, then there will be an imbalance of omega-3 and omega-6, which is never good.
- ➤ Margarine, coffee creamers and others with trans fats that increase the level of LDL cholesterol in your body, and eventually cause inflammation.

- Barley, rye and wheat, especially those suffering from celiac disease. Whole grains are otherwise good for everyone else.
- Excessive alcohol consumption.
- Soda, cookies, cakes, and sweets. They can easily cause high blood sugar, high cholesterol, and weight gain. Consumption of too much sugar releases inflammatory chemicals in the body known as cytokines. It is also good to limit the intake of honey and agave.

Does A Vegetarian Diet Reduce Inflammation?

This is an idea. In fact, several studies have been carried out to find out whether this works or not. And the evidence seems to suggest that inflammation can be reduced or even not appear at all if you become a vegetarian.

A study carried out in 2017 analyzed the data from 268 individuals who were on a strict vegetarian diet, and compared this with those eating non-veg foods. In the end, the researchers suggested that animal products do increase the risk of insulin resistance and systematic inflammation.

That is not all. Earlier, in 2014, researchers said that a vegan diet may also lower the levels of inflammation in the body.

AHA or the American Heart Association backs the vegan diet, saying that it is more **effective** (39) in preventing heart disease than their own previously recommended diet. They arrived at this conclusion after a study where 100 people with coronary artery disease were randomized to an AHA-recommended or vegan diet. They were followed for 8 weeks.

It was observed that high-sensitivity C-reactive protein, a marker for inflammation improved significantly in the group that was on the vegan diet.

The Public Health Nutrition journal published a report where it was also observed that a vegetarian diet can bring down inflammation. Here, the researchers looked at previously conducted 18 studies. They found that people eating a vegetarian diet for a minimum of 2 years were able to lower the serum levels of their C-reactive protein which is a biological marker of inflammation.

There was no such improvement in people that were not on a vegetarian diet. They noted that the improvement was because of the dietary fiber and phytosterols obtained from whole grains, legumes, vegetables, and fruits.

BONUS: HOW TO ACHIEVE WEIGHT LOSS WITH ANTI-INFLAMMATORY DIET

The anti-inflammatory diet doesn't promise to help you lose those excess pounds quickly. But it can still give great results, and there is real science behind it.

So how does it help you lose weight?

Basically, the diet involves avoiding starchy, high-fat, processed foods. You are encouraged to have natural foods where there are no artificial sweeteners or harmful chemicals. Eat fresh fruits, vegetables, poultry, fish, and whole grains, which are all very healthy. Restrict the intake of red meat, sugary substances, and alcohol.

Processed foods harm our body in many ways. Inflammation builds up, as this is your body's immune response to the toxins it detects.

Inflammation also causes food cravings. Fried foods, junk foods, red meat, refined grains, and sugar will not just lead to weight gain, but they will also increase our appetite as they are not nutritionally satisfying. Your body's requirements will not be met, so there will be heightened hunger, which will lead to overeating. Many fried, refined, and processed foods also have ingredients like MSG, sugar, excessive salt, and different chemicals that trigger a false sense of increased appetite.

On the other hand, anti-inflammatory foods like seeds, nuts, fruits, and green vegetables are extremely alkaline. They are the most nutrient-dense foods you will find. You will feel satisfied. Your body's nutritional requirements will be met. You won't overeat as a result.

Losing Weight with Anti-Inflammatory Foods

Natural foods do not trigger inflammatory responses in the body. This is why those on an anti-inflammatory diet show fewer instances of diabetes, cancer, heart disease, and obesity. These foods will make a huge difference, even if you are trying to shed only a few excess pounds. You will be able to digest better and have more energy.

You will feel full and won't overeat. This is the more sustainable way to manage weight as well as your body won't feel deprived. Your metabolism will increase as the body has to burn more fuel to digest natural foods.

Weight Gain and Neurological Inflammation

Recent clinical trials have indicated that neurological inflammation increases the set point weight that slows down metabolism, thereby causing weight gain.

This is how it works...

The hypothalamus, which controls our metabolism, is located in our brain. Insulin and leptin hormones regulate its function. A healthy hypothalamus will receive hormonal signals correctly. So your body will burn more calories when there is an increase. Your weight will balance automatically at the set point level. With a healthy hypothalamus, your set point level will not be elevated. In this situation, you won't have to worry about putting on weight or counting calories.

However, your hypothalamus will be inflamed if you have neurological inflammation. It won't receive the signals from your brain correctly. In this situation, your hormones and hypothalamus will hold on to fat instead of keeping you slim.

You can exercise and fast to reduce weight. But with neurological inflammation, it will be almost impossible for you to maintain it. The only option is to switch to an anti-inflammatory diet.

APPENDIX A:
MEASUREMENT CONVERSIONS

1 tablespoon = 3 teaspoons

4 tablespoons = 1/4 cup

1 ounce =2 tablespoons

1 cup = 8 oz.

8 oz. = ½ lb.

1 lb. = 2 cups

1 lb. = 16 oz.

1 tablespoon = 0.0326 lb.

31 tablespoons = 1.0106 lbs.

93 teaspoons = 1.0106 lb.

CONCLUSION

Thank you for purchasing this book and reading it.

Chronic inflammatory disease is a serious condition that cannot be neglected. Remember, it can cause poor health and even death.

Everyone is at risk. But a few simple foods and lifestyle changes can help. You will be able to reduce the risks and symptoms immensely.

I hope you have liked reading this book. Its time now to start preparing the recipes. Start with the ones you are comfortable with, and then maybe you can try a few new recipes. I have tried to include recipes with ingredients that you can easily get.

Share the recipes with your friends and family. Tell them of the need to switch to the anti-inflammatory diet. Better still, call them over, and show your cooking skills. Prepare food and eat together.

Happy cooking! Thank you and good luck!

REFERENCES

1. https://www.who.int/chp/chronic_disease_report/full_report.pdf

2. https://www.ncbi.nlm.nih.gov/pubmed?Db=pubmed&Cmd=ShowDetailView&TermToSearch=21195808

3. https://www.ncbi.nlm.nih.gov/pubmed?Db=pubmed&Cmd=ShowDetailView&TermToSearch=21195808

4. https://www.cancer.gov/about-cancer/causes-prevention/risk/chronic-inflammation

5. https://www.ncbi.nlm.nih.gov/pmc/articles/PMC5507106/

6. https://www.ncbi.nlm.nih.gov/pmc/articles/PMC5476783/

7. https://www.ncbi.nlm.nih.gov/pubmed/26526061

8. https://www.ncbi.nlm.nih.gov/pubmed/22176839

9. https://www.ncbi.nlm.nih.gov/pmc/articles/PMC5932180/

10. https://www.ncbi.nlm.nih.gov/pmc/articles/PMC2839879/

11. https://www.ncbi.nlm.nih.gov/pubmed/19295480

12. https://www.mdmag.com/medical-news/amy-tyberg-md-gerd-as-an-inflammatory-disease (

13. https://www.arthritis.org/health-wellness/healthy-living/nutrition/anti-inflammatory/anti-inflammatory-diet

14. https://www.ncbi.nlm.nih.gov/pubmed/24925270

15. https://www.ncbi.nlm.nih.gov/pubmed/24224694

16. https://www.ncbi.nlm.nih.gov/pubmed/26383493

17. https://www.ncbi.nlm.nih.gov/pmc/articles/PMC3629815/

18. https://www.ncbi.nlm.nih.gov/pubmed/26890214

19. https://www.ncbi.nlm.nih.gov/pubmed/20026349

20. https://www.cambridge.org/core/journals/nutrition-research-reviews/article/obesity-and-inflammation-the-effects-of-weight-loss/7DE5BD1B13C41487F6DE50B8DD19220F

21. https://www.ncbi.nlm.nih.gov/pubmed/24512603

22. https://doi.org/10.1080/10408398.2011.556759

23. https://www.ncbi.nlm.nih.gov/pubmed/26829184

24. https://www.ncbi.nlm.nih.gov/pubmed/21593509

25. https://www.ncbi.nlm.nih.gov/pmc/articles/PMC3022968/

26. https://doi.org/10.2174/1871530317666171114114321

27. https://www.ncbi.nlm.nih.gov/pubmed/20370896

28. https://www.tandfonline.com/doi/abs/10.1080/01635581.2012.650779

29. https://www.ncbi.nlm.nih.gov/pubmed/26088351

30. https://www.ncbi.nlm.nih.gov/pubmed/23543896

31. https://doi.org/10.1089/jmf.2011.0238

32. https://www.ncbi.nlm.nih.gov/pubmed/20231522

33. https://www.cell.com/cell/fulltext/S0092-8674(19)30850-5

34. https://www.cell.com/cell-metabolism/fulltext/S1550-4131(13)00454-3

35. https://www.ncbi.nlm.nih.gov/pubmed/24993615

36. https://www.hindawi.com/journals/jnme/2012/539426/

37. https://www.ncbi.nlm.nih.gov/pubmed/24552752

38. https://pubs.acs.org/doi/abs/10.1021/pr4008199

39. https://www.ahajournals.org/doi/10.1161/JAHA.118.011367

Made in the USA
Coppell, TX
28 May 2021

56500521R00152